The Ultimate Maldives Travel Guide 2024-2025

Things to Know before Travelling to Maldives, Expert picks for your Vacation, Top Things to do, Budget and Safety Tips

HILDA CATHY

Copyright

TABLE OF CONTENTS

INTRODUCTION 5

A brief overview of Maldives, its history, culture, and character..........5

Why visit Maldives in 2024? Top 10 Reasons to visit.......................18

CHAPTER ONE..27

Things to Know before you go to Maldives.................................27

THE 16 BEST Things to Do in Maldives- 2024 39

CHAPTER TWO 59

9 Best Maldives Festivals Not to Miss in 2024 59

Best Seasons to Visit Maldives: A Month-by-Month Guide 68

Essential Phrases to use in Maldives for Travelers and Tourists 73

CHAPTER THREE 79

Packing List: The Ultimate Maldives Packing List for Women & Men 79

CHAPTER FOUR 91

Getting Around in Maldives- A Guide for Getting Around in the City ..91

Best place to shop in Maldives 98

10 Best Things to Buy In Maldives 107

CHAPTER FIVE..117

Where To Stay in Maldives: Best Areas & Neighborhoods to Visit in Maldives 117

CHAPTER SIX..129

Best Luxury Hotels in Maldives 129

Best Boutique Hotels in Maldives 146

Best Cheap & Mid-range Hotels in Maldives 166

Best Hostels in Maldives 172

CHAPTER SEVEN 177

10 Must Eat Places in Maldives: Where to Eat in 2024....................177

Eat Like a Local in Maldives: 10 Must-Try Foods...........................186

The 12 Best Maldives Clubs & Bars 196

CHAPTER EIGHT..**207**

Best Maldives Beaches to Visit 207

Romantic Places in Maldives: Spots To Woo Your Partners...........215

Traveling on a Budget - Money Saving Tips.....................228

CHAPTER NINE..**233**

7 Days in Maldives: An Itinerary for First-Time Travelers................233

A BRIEF OVERVIEW OF MALDIVES, ITS HISTORY, CULTURE, AND CHARACTER

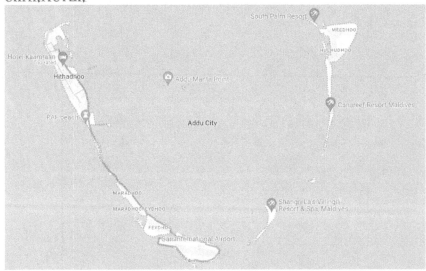

Located in the north-central Indian Ocean, the Maldives is an autonomous nation of islands. About 1,200 clusters, or atolls, of little coral islands and sandbanks make it up, with 200 of those islands being inhabited.

The length of the islands is over 510 miles (820 km) in the north-south direction and 80 miles (130 km) in the east-west direction. Approximately 370 miles (600 km) to the south-southwest of the Indian mainland is the northernmost atoll, while the center portion, which includes the capital island of Male (Male'), is situated approximately 400 miles (645 km) southwest of Sri Lanka.

Land

A buried old volcanic mountain range formed the foundation of the Maldives Islands, which are composed of a string of coral atolls. With the exception of one, not a single island rises more than six feet (1.8 meters) above sea level. The islands are shielded from the devastating monsoons by the barrier reefs. The southwest monsoon produces rain from May to August, whereas the northeast monsoon offers moderate breezes and dry conditions from December to March. An average of 76 to 86 degrees Fahrenheit (24 to 30 degrees Celsius) is experienced each year. Annual precipitation averages 84 inches (2,130 mm). The atolls are home to sandy beaches, lagoons, and an abundance of tropical flora, including breadfruit trees, tropical plants, and coconut palms. The reefs, lagoons, and waters around the islands are rich in fish, and sea turtles are harvested for both their meat and oil, which is used in traditional medicine.

People

As a consequence of many different peoples arriving on the islands of the Maldives throughout the course of its history, the Maldivian ethnic group makes up almost all of the population. It is often thought that the original inhabitants were Sinhalese and Tamils from southern India and Sri Lanka. Throughout history, the islands have been frequented by traders hailing from many Arab nations, as well as Malaya, Madagascar, Indonesia, and China. While Arabic, Hindi, and English are widely spoken, the official language is Dhivehi (or Maldivian), an Indo-European language. The religion of the state is Islam.

The percentage of people living in rural areas exceeds 50%. People in the Maldives mostly reside in tiny communities on islands in dispersed atolls, with the exception of the comparatively sizable population of males. The southern islands are more densely populated than their northern counterparts, and only about twenty of the islands have more than a thousand residents. The Maldives have a lower mortality rate and a slightly higher birth rate compared to the rest of the globe. People under the age of fifteen make up over 20% of the overall population. Men have a life expectancy of about 74 years and women have a life expectancy of around 79.

Economy

Fast economic growth has been a hallmark of the Maldives since the 1970s. With GDP growing at a rate of around 6% per year in the 2010s, the country's per capita gross national income (GNI) jumped from being among the world's lowest in the 1970s to being on par with upper middle-income nations by the end of that decade. Fishing, boatbuilding, and boat maintenance are the mainstays of the economy, with the tourist industry spearheading the impressive expansion.

Agriculture, forestry, and fishing

While fishing was once the backbone of the economy, tourism is now the engine that drives GDP growth. It employs less than 20% of the workforceand accounts for less than 10% of GDP, but it is still responsible for most of the country's exports and is still growing, although more slowly than the tourist industry. Although most of the fishing fleet has been automated, the pole-and-line technique is still widely used. used to catch tuna. Companies in other countries buy the majority of the fish caught and send it on to processing plants.

Even though the country's formal businesses have grown rapidly, particularly on the main islands, a large portion of the population still relies on fishing, gathering coconuts, and cultivating tropical fruits, vegetables, and roots and tubers like cassava, sweet potatoes, and yams. Because the cropland is so dispersed across so many little islands, almost all of the staple crops have to be imported.

Manufacturing

Fish canning, boatbuilding, and the production of coir (coconut-husk fiber) and coir goods are examples of the handicraft or cottage industries. In the mid-1990s, textile and garment manufacturing was a very successful industry. However, when the import quota system in international textile commerce expired in 2005, Maldives firms were no longer able to compete. Most manufacturing occurs in the construction industry.

Trade

In 2006, the Maldives became a member of SAFTA, and in 2017, they inked a free trade deal with China. Common consumer items that are imported include food (mostly rice), clothing, pharmaceuticals, and petroleum products. Most of the fish that is exported is skipjack tuna, either in its dry, frozen, or canned forms. Some of the most important commercial partners are China, India, the UAE, Thailand, Sri Lanka, and Singapore.

Services

Despite its nonexistence before 1972, the services sector is supported by the tourist industry. Over 1.5 million visitors go to the Maldives every year. You may stay in some of the world's most luxurious hotels on its 130+ resort islands, and you can enjoy scuba diving, water sports, underwater restaurants, and spas thanks to the area's diverse marine ecosystem. In the middle of the 2010s, the service sector was responsible for about 40% of the GDP.

Labour and taxation

A large number of people lost their jobs in agriculture and found work in the service sector as a result of the tourist industry's meteoric rise. Businesses rely on the expertise of South Asian immigrant workers, in part due to the general population's lack of training. Cultural norms restrict women from working away from home; therefore, their participation rate plummeted while firms on remote resort islands sought a larger proportion of the workforce. In the 1970s, almost 80% of women were working, but by the mid-1990s, that number had dropped to 20%. But the participation percentage had risen back up to almost 50% of women by the 2010s.

Businesses' and banks' earnings, as well as tourist-related products and services, were the main sources of revenue for the Maldives' tax system starting in 2011. In 2020, a tax on income was imposed.

Transportation

The nation's ability to transport its many islands and atolls is paramount. The strategically placed Maldives Islands are a flashpoint in the power struggle between China and India, which has led to substantial foreign direct investment in infrastructure development to further link the islands. Scheduled shipping routes connect the nation with Sri Lanka, Singapore, and India, and boats are the main mode of communication between the atolls. The national airline connects domestic and international airports for the benefit of its customers. Although other airports provide little international travel, the airport at Male handles the majority of foreign traffic.

Government and society

Constitutional framework

The Maldives' constitution came into effect in 2008. The President, with the help of the Vice President and the Cabinet, serves as the chief executive and head of state. With the use of universal suffrage, the president and vice president are elected directly to staggered five-year terms. In addition to the president and ministers, the cabinet also includes the attorney general. With the exception of the vice president, the president chooses every member of the cabinet.

The People's Majlis, the unicameral legislature, convenes three times a year. From Male Island and each of the twenty atoll groups that split the nation administratively, its members are chosen for five-year terms. Each administrative division has a minimum of two delegates, with the number of representatives being decided by the population. The state religion of Islam was declared in the 2008 constitution. It is forbidden for the People's Majlis to pass any legislation that goes against the principles of Islam, and non-Muslims cannot become citizens. Commissions on civil service and human rights are two further examples of government agencies.

Justice

The Supreme Court is the highest court in the country. The president nominates or elects ten members to the Judicial Service Commission, which advises him on the appointment of judges. The Judicial Service Commission appoints each additional judge on an impartial basis. The retirement age is 70 and there are no limitations on the number of terms a judge may serve. Sunni Muslims must constitute the judiciary. The Supreme Court takes into account Shariah (Islamic law) in situations where Maldives law and the constitution are irrelevant. Additionally, there are trial courts and the High Court.

Health and welfare

Concerns about cardiovascular disease, cancer, diabetes, and kidney failure are the most common. Hepatitis and typhoid are only two examples of the food- and water-borne diseases that pose a small but real threat. After successfully eliminating malaria in 1984, the Maldives became the first nation in the area to get the World Health Organization's certification of being malaria-free in 2015.

Every inhabited island has a basic health center, no matter how big or small the population is. Atolls usually have a larger facility or hospital on the main island. On the other hand, Maldivians with more severe illnesses need to go to Male for treatment.

Education

Traditional schools (makthabs) in the Maldives educate students on how to read and recite the Qur'an. Other options include schools taught in Dhivehi and elementary and secondary schools taught in English. The only schools that provide secondary education and follow a conventional curriculum are those that speak English as their primary language. Enrollment reduces dramatically for upper secondary education; however, almost all children between the ages of 6 and 15 are enrolled in elementary or lower secondary A small number of private institutions offer higher education. Before a small number of degree programs were made accessible later on, the first public institution to offer a bachelor's degree program in the Maldives was the Maldives National University (previously the Maldives College of Higher Education), which opened in 2000. To get the majority of degrees, Maldivians have to study overseas.

History of Maldives

The Buddhist inhabitants of the archipelago, who likely originated in southern India and Sri Lanka, settled there around the fifth century BCE. Traditional accounts date the adoption of Islam to 1153 CE. The independence of the women, which has been visible throughout Maldivian history, was remarked upon disapprovingly by Ibn Battuta, a famous North African explorer who lived there in the mid-1340s and recorded the situation at that time.

The Portuguese colonized Male against their will from 1558 until they were expelled in 1573. After the Dutch gained control of Ceylon (now Sri

Lanka) in 1796, the islands became a sultanate under their protection. In 1887, the British formally recognized the islands as a protectorate. Prior to the proclamation of the first democratic constitution in 1932, the majority of administrative functions were held by sultans, or sultanas, and the nation continued to be a sultanate. In 1953, the nation was officially declared a republic, although it returned to a sultanate later that same year.

After declaring complete independence from Britain in 1965, the Maldives Islands dissolved the sultanate and formed a republic in 1968. Independence Day in the Maldives is commemorated annually on March 29, 1976, the day of the last British soldiers' departure. Maumoon Abdul Gayoom replaced Ibrahim Nasr as president in 1978 and was re-elected to a sixth consecutive term in 2003. Although it renounced its membership from 2016 to 2020 due to a political dispute, the Maldives re-joined the Commonwealth in 1982. Near Indonesia in the Indian Ocean, a tremendous earthquake in December 2004 produced a huge tsunami that ravaged the Maldives. A large number of lives were lost and several pieces of property were destroyed.

The administration of Gayoom set out in the early years of this century on a grand strategy to democratize and modernize the Maldives, focusing on the country's political and economic systems. Another flaw with the country's judicial system was pointed out in the proposal. To improve the system of government and human rights, extensive changes were started in 2003. A system of many political parties was established. There are now more checks and balances in governance, the legislative and judiciary have more authority, and women may run for president thanks to a new constitution that was approved in 2008. In October of that year, the country's first multicandidate presidential election took place; Gayoom's 30-year rule came to an end with the victory of Mohamed Nasheed, a former political prisoner.

Since Nasheed believed that the low-lying islands were in grave danger from increasing sea levels, combating climate change was one of his top goals. But the legislature and the judiciary's steadfast devotion to Gayoom constituted a problem for his government. The detention of a senior judge from the criminal court by Nasheed caused a stir in January 2012. After weeks of protests by citizens opposed to the arrest, Nasheed resigned as president in early February, and Mohamed Waheed Hassan took over as president. The police and the military, Nasheed said, coerced him into resigning. He was indicted in July on accusations related to what was believed to have been his unlawful detention of the judge of the criminal court in January. There was no coup and Nasheed's resignation was voluntary, according to an official commission of investigation supported by the Commonwealth in August.

The political turmoil surrounding Nasheed's resignation and its circumstances persisted, leaving his legal standing uncertain. Nasheed narrowly defeated the second-place candidate in the September 2013 general election, although he was still not elected with a majority of the vote. Abdulla Yameen Abdul Gayoom, who is half the brother of Maumoon Abdul Gayoom, narrowly defeated Nasheed in a subsequent election that took place in November. In 2015, Nasheed was given a 13-year jail term. His request to go to the United Kingdom for medical care was approved. January 2016 before making his escape to Sri Lanka. But in late 2018, just days after the Supreme Court reversed his conviction, he came back to the nation.

Although Yameen's administration did not possess the charm of Gayoom, it was responsible for supervising major infrastructural projects in the nation. To the dismay of China's long-standing partner, India, the Chinese government footed the bill for most of the projects. Aside from that, Yameen imprisoned political opponents and silenced critics. Following the Supreme Court's decision to reverse the sentences of several political opponents of Yameen in February 2018, he proceeded to imprison two judges of the court and proclaimed a 45-day state of emergency. Many people thought that September's election would be used to solidify Yameen's dictatorship. But the opposition banded together to depose Yameen, and they fielded only one candidate: Nasheed's close associate and senior lawmaker, Ibrahim Mohamed Solih. With over 90% of the eligible voters casting ballots, Solih unexpectedly won the election by a wide margin. At first, Yameen admitted defeat and praised Solih. A few weeks later, Yameen changed her mind and petitioned the Supreme Court to look into allegations of vote fraud and election manipulation; however, the court found no proof of misconduct and maintained the outcome of the election.

The handover of power was finalized on November 17 with Solih's sworn-in into office. When his party won three-quarters of the seats in the legislature in April 2019, he was even more solidified. The People's Majlis unanimously chose Nasheed as speaker the month after. The current administration has launched investigations into corruption and human rights violations committed by the previous administration. The November conviction of Yameen on accusations of money-laundering was the consequence of one inquiry; nevertheless, the overturning of the verdict occurred two years later. Solih also made an effort to strengthen the country's relationship with India. The Maldives were the destination of Indian Prime Minister Narendra Modi's first foreign trip after his re-election in June 2019, a move that suggested a desire to improve relations between the two countries. Under Solih's watch, India has promised the Maldives over $2 billion in assistance, with half of that amount going toward a massive infrastructure project that would connect Male and the surrounding islands.

Despite efforts to combat corruption and other structural issues, including religious extremism and political violence, the administration faced persistent hurdles. After months of medical care overseas, Nasheed returned to the People's Majlis in October 2021 after his catastrophic injuries sustained in May 2021 when an improvised explosive device detonated outside his residence.

WHY VISIT MALDIVES IN 2024? TOP 10 REASONS TO VISIT

There is an endless supply of reasons to visit the Maldives, with its over a thousand beautiful islands and 26 coral atolls teeming with marine life, incredible diving, and pristine white sand beaches. Here are 10 of them

1. Relax On the Beaches

One of the nicest things about visiting the Maldives is the opportunity to relax on the beaches while enjoying the breathtaking view of the emerald-green Indian Ocean stretching out into the distance. The mornings are lovely, with gentle sunbeams and gentler waves, but the twilight hours, with their many shades of purple, crimson, and orange, are really enchanted. In a climate that never drops below 25 or 30 degrees Celsius, relax to the sound of the waves and the salt air. Reimagine love under a sky filled with millions of stars.

2. Swim With the Sharks

A lot of people go to the Maldives to see the reef sharks and the spectacular whale sharks that live in the coral atolls and lagoons around the different resorts. The atolls of Baa and Ari, as well as Maaya Thila, are potential near-encounter locations for these sharks, although they are native to the region. They are also rather predictable when it comes to their daily feeding time, which you can see at some resorts.

3. Dive Into the Coral Reef

Another top incentive to visit the Maldives is to do deep sea diving or snorkeling and see marine life, including barracuda, sea turtles, and manta rays, that swims through the colorful coral reef. Visit Kuda Huraa if you want to swim in warm water that won't make you wear a wetsuit. You should either use a waterproof camera or carry a protective cover for your camera since reef fish are friendly.

4. Enjoy Water Sports

One of the top ten reasons to go to the Maldives is to enjoy water activities like jet skiing, snorkeling, kayaking, canoeing, sea bobbing, rollerblading (X-Jet Blades), etc. No matter your skill level, the best resorts usually have instructors available to help you out. Additionally, you should add the dolphin and turtle safari boats to your bucket list. Sunshine, monsoon breezes, and regular waves make atolls like Laamu Atoll perfect for surfers of all skill levels. Doing water sports in the Maldives is, without a doubt, a must-do when visiting the nation.

5. Cherish Maldivian Culture

The Maldives is well-known not just for its stunning landscapes and historical landmarks but also for its lively culture. Be sure to see Bodu Beru, the famous Maldivian folk dance, performed nightly on the beach if you want to learn fascinating things about the Maldives. You have the option to either film the event or get down and dirty with the dancers. Getting to know the locals and their culture while cruising the Maldives aboard a Dhoni may be just as delightful.

6. Relish The Cuisine

In case you're still wondering, "Why go to the Maldives?" This should do the trick. Enjoying traditional Maldivian cuisine, such as Maldivian curry with tuna, while lounging on the beach in the Maldives is a big draw for many tourists. Seafood dishes such as Garudhiya, a fish soup with lime, chili, rice, curry leaves, onions, and a coconut, are perfect for indulging in freshly caught seafood. Street foods such as Mas Kashi, dried fish with mango and coconut; Hedhika, which combines tuna, egg, potato, and coconut; and Mashumi Roshi, tuna and chapati, are all delicious.

7. Get Spa Therapy

The Maldives are famous for their spa treatments; that much is certain. Rejuvenating one's body, mind, and spirit with luxurious spa treatments is the Maldives' claim to fame. If you're not a fan of the typical beach cabana massage, you should definitely check out the underwater Huvafen Fushi. As the therapist works her reiki magic on you, you can't tear your eyes away from the breathtaking panorama of the resort's house reef and its abundant marine life. As you drink ginger tea and enjoy a foot massage or full-body therapeutic treatment at the Kuda Huraa, you can also see marine life through the glass floor panels of the treatment rooms.

8. Watch Bioluminescent Water Under the Stars

Visit Vaadhoo Island in Raa Atoll to see stars envious of the Indian Ocean's playful sea of stars as you question, "What is so great about the Maldives?" As the waves pass by, phytoplankton dinoflagellates release their glowing poisons as a defense mechanism against predatory fish and other marine animals. Despite their unscientific nature, it's clear that you can stroll through them to make a lasting impression with even greater luminosity.

9. Visit The Architectural Heritages

With its shimmering golden dome, Arabic calligraphy, wood carvings on the walls, and library, the Grand Friday Mosque at the Islamic Center dominates the skyline of Male. It is also the biggest mosque in the Maldives. Another major reason to visit the Maldives is to observe the finely carved wooden door and side panels, exquisite chandeliers, and carpet. Come between 2 and 3 in the afternoon to avoid the crowds and get a chance to explore. Additional noteworthy instances of coral stonework may be seen at the Friday Mosques of Meedhoo, Ihavandhoo, Male Eid, Isdhoo Old, and Fenfushi. The Hukuru Miskiiy, renowned for its intricate carvings of wood, coral, and lacquer, should not be overlooked. Of all the fascinating locations to visit in the Maldives, the country's architectural heritage monuments are without a doubt the most popular.

10. Explore Male And suburbs

Even though many people are drawn to the concept of a carefree island lifestyle, many people feel that the Maldives, namely Male and its suburbs, embody the authentic Maldivian way of life. At Villingili, you can see the royal bath and jail, and at Hulhumale, you may swim among the fish in the coral atolls. Another option is to hire a scooter and ride it around Male's less-traveled areas.

Visit Male's thriving fruit and seafood market to stock up on seasonal produce. You may witness the fishermen bringing in their catch if you go in the morning. Spend some money on papaya, mango, coconut, watermelon, dried fish, etc., or visit the Maldives' oldest industry—fishing.

CHAPTER ONE

THINGS TO KNOW BEFORE YOU GO TO MALDIVES

The Maldives are a popular vacation spot, and who among us hasn't dreamed about going there? The archipelago is home to over a thousand little islands surrounded by pristine waters, making it a top pick among honeymooners worldwide. Planning a vacation to the Maldives can be a real headache, and there are many myths and misunderstandings surrounding this island paradise. To help clear the air, we've compiled all the information you'll need before your trip.

"The Maldives" is made up of almost 1,200 small islands

The Maldives, an archipelago of islands in the Indian Ocean, is often mentioned when discussing this area. The 26 natural atolls that make up the little islands extend over 800 kilometers in a north-south direction.

Male (or Malé) is the capital of the Maldives, and the majority of foreign tourists' land at Velana International Airport. Although the Maldives encompasses around 90,000 square kilometers, its land area is less than 300 square kilometers, making it the ninth-smallest nation in the world. About 200 of these islands are inhabited, while another 200 serve as resort islands.

No, you don't need a visa

No visa is needed to enter the Maldives before you arrive. Every nationality is granted a 30-day visa upon arrival; nevertheless, it is essential that you possess a valid exit ticket out of the Maldives and that your passport retains a minimum of six months of validity.

You cannot bring alcohol into the Maldives

It is against the law to import alcoholic beverages into the Maldives. You may retrieve any alcoholic beverages you purchased at a duty-free store on your departure from the Maldives; however, you must leave them with customs upon arrival. Any of the inhabited islands in the Maldives prohibit the sale and consumption of alcoholic beverages due to the country's Islamic religion.

Islam is the official religion of the Maldives

The great majority of Maldivians are Sunni Muslims, who were brought to the island nation at the tail end of the 12th century. You could hear the calls to prayer all day long if you stay near a mosque, and nearby islands don't allow pork or alcohol.

Wearing modest clothing (no bikinis or revealing tops are allowed unless you're at a designated "bikini beach") and avoiding public displays of love are all good ways to demonstrate respect for local Maldivian culture. On an island reserved for private resorts, it is quite acceptable to wear a bikini.

Peak season is from early December to March

The weather is tropical, with daily highs of 28–30 degrees Celsius, although the monsoon season (April–October), especially the months of June and August, sees a dramatic increase in rainfall. Because of this, the months of December through March are peak tourism seasons in the Maldives, and hotel rates reflect this.

While we did witness a few storms during our July vacation to the Maldives—the "monsoon season"—the majority of our days were sunny and breezy. My tan is definitely visible! Going to the Maldives in the off-season has many advantages, such as cheaper costs and fewer tourists.

Keep an eye on the dates of the Islamic festival of Eid Al-Adha as well; the Maldives is a popular destination for vacationers during that week and may be rather crowded. The event is held on a different day each year in accordance with the Islamic lunar calendar.

The peak surf season is the opposite

During the monsoon season in June, July, or August—the height of surfing—the Maldives are the place to go if you're a serious surfer seeking the biggest waves of the year. If you're an intermediate surfer looking for the Maldives in the shoulder seasons of April, May, September, or October, you'll find somewhat less scary waves and fewer crowds.

Although some of the breakers in the Maldives are private and require special permission, the country is nevertheless a top-tier surfing destination with hundreds of breaks. Another option would be to gather a group of buddies and rent a boat to reach the more isolated reef breaks.

Get used to "Island Time"

It's not out of the ordinary for hotels to be an extra hour or two ahead of Male's official time. It may take a few days to adjust to the resort's "island time" in order to maximize the amount of time spent in the sun, but after that, you'll probably stop caring about the passage of time.

Choosing a hotel can be overwhelming

Here's some good news: you're not stuck staying at resorts that charge $1,000 a night; there are lots of other possibilities. Because there are so many atolls, each with an incomprehensible name that doesn't tell you where it is, choosing a hotel might be a real challenge.

What atoll would you recommend seeing? Which is better: a private resort or a guesthouse on a nearby island? Which is more practical: a hotel that is accessible by seaplane or one that is accessible by speedboat? Would you want a property on the beach or one that overlooks the water?

You should definitely stay near the airport if you're trying to stick to a tight budget. This makes it easy to reach the nearby guesthouse by shared boat or private speedboat. Be sure to factor in the time and money required to go to the resort, as well as the cost of transportation and taxes, while comparing the many Maldives hotel alternatives on websites like Booking.com. With just three days to see the Maldives, taking a seaplane and then a 45-minute boat voyage may not be the best use of your time.

After a short seaplane ride (about 35 minutes) from the airport, we headed north to the Lhaviyana Atoll to stay at the magnificent Kanuhura Maldives, which is now known as Six Senses Kanuhura. The breathtaking beach-chic décor at Kanuhura had us in awe, and we like boutique hotels that provide a touch of the extraordinary.

Two more quiet, uninhabited islands are available to you at Kanuhura for your perfect beach getaway. Kanuhura is one of the greatest boutique hotels in the Maldives, and if you wish to stay in a bungalow or villa there without taking out a mortgage, you will have the beach vacation of a lifetime. Alternatively, island resorts in the Maldives sometimes have flash sales of 40–70% off nightly prices on sites like Secret Escapes and Luxury Escapes, so it's a great time to shop around.

You don't have to stay in an overwater villa to enjoy the Maldives

Yeah, you heard it correctly! Listen, an overwater house isn't necessary for a fantastic Maldives vacation. Our private pool and sunset beach villa were perfect, and we enjoyed waking up every morning to the sound of the waves lapping at the door.

Plus, it provides a lot more shelter from the rain and wind. The misconception that all Maldives accommodations must be overwater villas should not dissuade you from planning a vacation there.

Seaplanes are AMAZING

I've never been on a seaplane, but I have been in a lot of aircraft, helicopters, and propeller jets. Trust me when I say this: it is an unforgettable experience. From Male International Airport, a round-trip ticket might cost anything from $200 to $500, but the sights are well worth the price.

Make sure to include your seaplane travel plans when you book your accommodation. Demand determines the seaplanes' timetable, and you won't receive confirmation of your flight time until the night before your arrival. So, don't worry if you don't know your flight time a week in advance.

You could have to hang about in Kanuhura's incredible private waiting area until other people show up, and seaplanes can get stuck in the rain because they can't see the runway. Since seaplanes are unable to fly after dark, you will need to make other arrangements for your overnight stay in Male if your arrival is in the evening.

The Maldives has outrageously cool marine life

Marine life in the Maldives is really astounding, including over a thousand different fish species, forty different shark species, dolphins, turtles, tropical fish, manta rays, sting rays, sea turtles, and whale sharks, among many other incredible creatures. While the coral reef and diving opportunities here are second to none, visitors should be aware that the marine ecosystem is becoming more precarious as a result of human activities like overfishing, climate change, pollution, and others.

The islands of the Maldives are only 1-2 meters above sea level, making them very vulnerable to the consequences of global warming. There are many things you can do to help, such as utilizing public transportation, decreasing your use of single-use plastic, helping with beach cleanups, and reusing towels instead of throwing them away.

Go to the Marine Biology Research Centre on Kanuhura if you're interested in Maldives conservation. Coral reef ecology, preservation, and research are its primary focuses, and it also assists in getting the word out about ocean conservation efforts in the surrounding areas.

Taking seashells with you is illegal

Unbeknownst to many, the Maldives have very stringent regulations against the collection of seashells, sand, coral, and tortoise shells. Hermit crabs, who build their nests in shells, are responsible for controlling a sizable portion of the sand fly population.

Impressive internet connectivity

Ooredoo Tourist Rate Packs				
Tourist Packs	Your Tourist Pack $15	Your Tourist Pack $20	Your Tourist Pack $30	Your Tourist Pack $50
Price (USD)	15	20	30	50
Free Data	4 GB	17 GB	17 GB	30 GB
Free Local Minutes	50	75	150	300
Free Local SMS	50 SMS	75 SMS	150 SMS	300 SMS
Free Credit	-	-	100 MVR	150 MVR
Excess Data	1 Laari/ KB			
IDD SMS	1 MVR/ Min			
IDD Calls Charge	IDD Normal rate			
Local Calls	1.5 MVR/ Min			
Local SMS	20 Laari/ SMS			
Validity	7 Days		14 Days	

You could anticipate fairly spotty internet access given the islands' isolated position. Nonetheless, it's not terrible! At the airport, you may get a local SIM card with 4 GB of data for $15 USD or 17 GB of data for $20 USD. The internet at a private resort should be reliable and accessible in every accommodation and public space.

THE 16 BEST THINGS TO DO IN MALDIVES- 2024

Water sports, romance, and exciting adventures are what the Maldives are all about. We spent our time in the Maldives on two private islands, but we made the most of our time there by taking day excursions to nearby atolls and the capital, Male. Regardless of your interests, these are the top Maldives activities!

1. Scuba Diving

It doesn't matter whether you're an experienced diver or have never dove a fin; the Maldives are among the world's top dive spots. Some of the top attractions in the Maldives include coral reefs, wrecks, and colorful marine life, including harmless white tip reef sharks, which may be best seen from the water's surface.

In order to have the greatest visibility, scuba divers should go during the dry season, which lasts from January to April. You may still go scuba diving in the other months if there aren't any major storms that are causing the waves to rise and fall.

In a similar vein, scuba diving is available at almost every major resort on the islands. There are whole resorts built on scuba diving in the area around South Male Atoll, which is home to some of the greatest spots. An on-site PADI diving facility is available at the Fihalhohi Island Resort, which may be booked online. You want to give scuba diving a go, but you're a complete novice. This diving exploration trip will pick you up from your hotel or rental near Maafushi Island, provide you with the necessary equipment, and demonstrate how it works in a safe atmosphere with experienced instructors.

2. Visit Your Own Private Island

Perfect beaches and five-star hotels are available in many parts of the globe. We're picturing the Greek Islands, the Caribbean, and Hawaii. However, what's missing from that place? A whole private island where your hotel or home is the only building on the whole island.

One of the rarest locations on Earth where you may discover such lodgings is the Maldives. A cab will not be waiting for you when you disembark from your aircraft at Male International Airport. The only item at your ultimate destination is your resort; therefore, you'll be traveling by specially chartered aircraft or ship, maybe with other incoming guests.

Usually, the resort itself arranges seaplane transfers to the sandy beaches of private island resorts. In about half an hour, you can reach ultra-luxury resorts like the Four Seasons Landaa Giraavaru, all while taking in the breathtaking view of fifty different colors of blue from above. A personal hideaway on your very own island, most accommodations come with their very own swimming pool. You may reach hotels closer to Male by speedboat if a seaplane trip doesn't appeal to your sense of relaxation. Gliding over the turquoise waters, the COMO Cocoa Island Resort (bookable online) is just forty minutes from the airport.

Do you intend to accomplish monumental feats? Even more extravagant is the Waldorf Astoria Maldives Ithaafushi, a mega-luxury resort. Reserve their private island and enjoy complete seclusion on an oceanfront playground. Enjoy one of the three island villas, individualized service for meals and activities, and complete seclusion from the outside world.

3. Explore Malé City

Although most visitors go directly to the resort islands, Malé, the capital city, is worth seeing for a few hours. The vibrant structures, lively street life, and hypnotic mosques of this city on a small part of North Male Atoll have brought it international fame.

One of the best sites to visit in the Maldives before getting back to regular life, it's less than 10 minutes away from the Maldives International Airport. A third of the population lives in Male City, making it one of the most densely inhabited cities in the world.

The compactness of the area, which accounts for its high population, makes it simple to explore in a few hours. For that reason, it is a popular rest point for tourists heading out of the nation.

Two of Male's most famous landmarks, the Old Friday Mosque and the Male Fish Market, will be covered in detail in the sections that follow. The sights and sounds of ordinary life in this island country are on display, including a surf break, stingray spots, and inhabitants enjoying beach volleyball and cricket.

This walking tour of Male, the capital city, is a good place to start if you're not sure what to see or do first. The tour guides could be men or women. It is designed to be done during your stopover before you depart from the Maldives, and it even includes transportation from the airport. There is an extra charge for luggage storage.

4. National Museum, Maldives

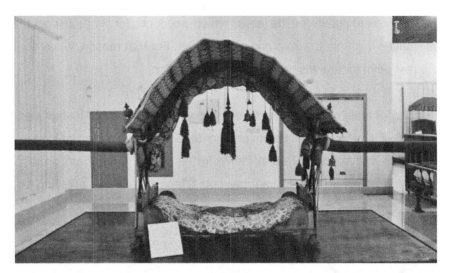

Visit the National Museum of the Maldives if you want to have a deeper understanding of the Maldives' distinctive culture and history. Originally inaugurated on November 11, National Day of the Maldives, 1952, the museum now serves as a national patriotic focal point.

The museum's collection of antiquities spans two eras: the Islamic monarchy and the Buddhist period. An etched wooden board from the thirteenth century, garments woven in the fifteenth century, and a Buddha head from the eleventh century are among the most important and ancient objects. It contains manuscripts made of fabric and paper that date back to the beginning of Maldivian history.

Even though most people go to the Maldives to relax on the beach, it's worthwhile to explore the country's culture and history outside the resorts to really understand the locals. Whether you're in Male City for a day trip or just want to see something before you go, the museum is the perfect spot to do it.

To visit all of the exhibits on the museum's two floors, it will take around an hour.

Address: National Museum, 5GG6+V3C, Chaandhanee Magu, Malé, Maldives

5. Swim With Whale Sharks

The magnificent whale shark is among the most stunning marine animals, and not only in the Maldives. Many go to the Maldives in the hopes of witnessing these placid giants up close and maybe even swimming with them.

Whale sharks, which may reach a length of more than 60 feet, are the biggest fish species currently known to humans. However, you shouldn't be scared off by their size or moniker. Because of their sluggish movement and ability to filter feed, whale sharks do not represent a hazard to swimmers.

A whale shark encounter may be arranged with the aid of most hotels, particularly in the South Ari Atoll. Another option is to plan a five-day trip to South Ari Atoll that covers everything from lodging to meals to a whale shark encounter. Part of the journey will also include seeing sandbanks and manta rays.

Rent a speedboat and go to nearby Maafushi if you'd rather do it yourself. A dolphin, whale shark, and manta ray boat excursion with a picnic on the beach is available from that point on. To save money on your trip, this is the way to go.

6. Have an Underwater Spa Day

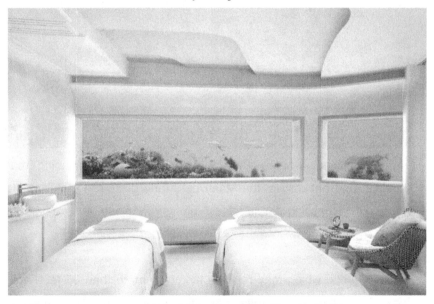

A spa treatment on a tropical island is the ultimate holiday experience. With the wide variety of high-end spas offered by the Maldives' five-star hotels, this is a popular activity for couples visiting the archipelago.

In the Maldives, there is more than one top attraction; what if you could combine a relaxing spa day with another? There is no other location on Earth that can match the sensation of the Huvafen Fushi resort's underwater spa. As you relax with a massage, you may look out over the vibrant reef and its inhabitants.

You will be eight meters (approximately 26 feet) below ground in the therapy chamber. Underwater Rendezvous lasts 120 minutes and Underwater Dream is 60 or 90 minutes long; both treatments are tailored to maximize the space. Both are full-body compositions that will make you feel as light as a feather and completely at peace.

Even if you're not turning the fish green with envy in the treatment room, the Huvafen Fushi has several advantages above ground. Among the many facilities offered by this stunning island are beach and overwater bungalows, an infinity pool, many dining options, and an overwater fitness center.

Address: North Malé Atoll, 08390, Maldives

7. Sultan Park

We have established that Male is one of the world's most densely inhabited cities. Its little landmass is crammed end-to-end with buildings and cranes as soon as you drive over the bridge from the airport. Sultan Park is a great spot to get away from the city without having to go to an outside island. Squeezed into a seemingly little spot in the city's center-north, its verdant gardens give the impression of much more room than there really is.

Before its destruction in the 1600s, the park stood on the site of the Royal Palace. As it is now, it is home to hundreds of plants and trees, a number of sculptures and fountains, and an abundance of benches and other seating areas away from the hustle and bustle of the city.

You may not be visiting the Maldives with the express purpose of visiting a park, but if you find yourself in the city for the day, this may be a beautiful place to see typical Maldivian leisure. Visitors from other countries are required to pay a nominal charge of around $5 in order to access the park.

Address: 5GH6+2C2, Male, Maldives

8. Snorkel With Manta Rays

The atolls of the Maldives are teeming with amazing marine life, as we hope has become evident by now. The islands are also home to magnificent manta rays, another animal that shouldn't be missed. Unlike the more well-known stingrays, mantas have wing-shaped fins instead of a spherical body. While swimming along the shore, they filter feed on little plankton with their wide-open jaws and short tails.

Popular areas in the Maldives, particularly in and around South Male Atoll, are good places to see them. To go to these spots and maybe swim with them, often in big schools, sign up for a guided snorkeling excursion. I could have spent hours observing these serene animals, according to most swimmers who attempt this.

While seeing manta rays is certainly the highlight of many of these excursions, keep in mind that you will also likely encounter many other species of exotic marine life. Although the thought of seeing a shark—whether a white-tip or gray reef shark—may strike fear into your heart, rest assured that these fish are really very placid and won't cause you any trouble. A bonus is that you can brag to your friends and family about swimming with sharks.

Address: Maafushi Ferry, WFVQ+7RG, Maafushi, Maldives

9. Male Fish Market

At the northern end of the island, near the port, you'll find Male, home to one of the few free activities in the Maldives. You may peruse the day's haul and stock up on delicious seafood at the Male Fish Market.

Tuna, sailfish, and reef fish, among other fresh catches, will be laid out by local fishermen. Though you'll notice more activity if you go early in the day, you may catch fish at any time of day at the fish market.

This is the Maldives' primary marketplace for fresh produce, including fish. A large portion of this country's land is unsuitable for farming; hence, a significant portion of the food supply is imported. Everyone, from hotels and restaurants to regular folks, may find everything they need for their kitchens here.

The fish market is just one of many stops on our walking tour of Male's must-see attractions. If you want to purchase refreshments or souvenirs, you'll need cash.

Address: 188 Ibrahim Hassan Didi Magu, Male, 20188, Maldives

10. Banana Reef

Banana Reef, a crescent-shaped coral reef off the shore of the airport, was the earliest and most renowned diving spot in the Maldives.

Because of its easy accessibility and remarkable aquatic environment, it is deserving of a placement on our list.

Caves, overhangs, cliffs, and walls are just some of the seabed features you might discover in Banana Reef. You may see sharks, manta rays, huge groupers, and a variety of colorful reef species in the vicinity. While scuba divers may get the greatest view of the reef by descending, snorkelers can get a great overview of the whole area just by floating above it.

Both the city and the resorts in the North Malé Atoll region provide easy access to the site. Located to the east of the airport, the stunning Sheraton Maldives Full Moon Resort & Spa is the closest hotel. Several restaurants, stunning bungalows with pools, and a prime location for exploring Male are all available here.

11. Tour a Local Island

Indeed, the private resort islands are very breathtaking. You may be surprised to learn that the average Maldivian does not spend their days lounging beneath palm trees in overwater bungalows. Day trips to one of the numerous nearby islands will give you a feel for real Maldivian living. Maldivians live, work, and play on a little more than 200 of the more than 1,000 islands that comprise this enormous nation.

An island resort like the Meeru Island Resort & Spa, which is adjacent to a nearby island, is one possibility. The little island of Dhiffushi is situated immediately across a short canal from the Meeru Island Resort. From the resort, you may reach the hamlet via water taxi, which you can then use to explore.

To avoid day trips altogether, another option is to get a room on a nearby island. On the island of Maafushi, for instance, you'll find the Arena Beach Hotel, which is a favorite spot for island visitors and may be reserved here. The residents are famously friendly and accommodating to tourists, and the island's relaxed ambiance gives it the feel of a fishing hamlet.

Finally, one of the two international airports in the country (the other being Male-Gan) may be worth considering if you're seeking to be more imaginative with your schedule. Before boarding a plane from Gan International Airport, you may want to explore this picturesque island, which is home to a sizable portion of the country's population. The best way to really immerse yourself in the local culture is to book a vacation rental.

12. Sunset Cruise

As the sun sets over the breathtaking Maldives, it becomes even more of a romantic and idyllic way to wind out the day. The experience may be elevated to a whole new level when done from a boat during a sunset cruise.

Evening boat trips to watch the sun go down are available from a number of islands in the area, including several of the resort islands. One way to identify them in the generally alcohol-free Maldives is that they provide light appetizers or supper together with tropical cocktails and other alcoholic drinks.

Pre- or post-sunset activities are available on several of these cruises. Night fishing is available on this sunset trip from Huraa or Dhiffushi, and the outfit includes all you need to reel in a monster catch while stargazing. Once you've had a fantastic day exploring the sandbanks and marine life on this snorkeling trip, you'll be able to relax on board until dusk.

Make sure to schedule evenings to watch the sunset from your resort's beach in addition to going on a sunset cruise to fully appreciate the breathtaking hues of the Maldives sky at night. No matter where you're going to view the sunset, you should definitely have a nice camera to record the occasion.

13. Go Surfing

The Maldives could be your best bet for finding that ideal wave. Though the waves in the Maldives aren't as well-known as those in Indonesia or Hawaii, those who have surfed there have raved about how much fun it is.

The monsoon season has an impact on the surfing season in the Maldives, which runs from April to October. On the other hand, ideal ocean conditions may manifest at any time of year. The necessary southeastern swell produces small to medium waves with lengthy, even breaks.

That being said, unlike the north coast of Maui, this is more of a place where novices may go surfing. However, you should be cautious since the Maldives' bottoms are typically reefs. Going out on a tour or even just asking a local for advice is your best bet.

On the inhabited islands, you can find surf stores that can provide you with gear and guidance. If you don't have a board with you, you could be lucky enough to get one at a hotel. You'll be happy you got on the water while you're grooving to tunes on scenic breaks while distant atolls add to the beauty.

14. Dolphin Watching

The Maldives are home to dolphins, one of the most beloved aquatic animals on Earth. The islands are home to around 20 different kinds of dolphins, including spinner and spotted dolphins.

Many day cruises go out in search of dolphins, and most of the time, they are successful in doing so since seeing dolphins is so popular. Departing in the late afternoon, this Dhiffushi dolphin cruise heads to the atoll's edge, a popular spot for aquatic mammals. As they playfully swim and leap about the boat, the dolphins often put on a spectacular display for the tourists.

This Maafushi tour will take your dolphin viewing to the next level by allowing you to snorkel with the dolphins. As an added bonus, you'll get to swim alongside majestic trevallies and nurse sharks, and you'll even get underwater video and images, which you're sure to desire after an adventure like this.

15. Tsunami Monument

Tourists will find the Maldives to be a beach paradise, but they should be aware that the country's composition of tiny atolls makes it vulnerable to certain natural catastrophes that have caused loss of life in the past. Many of us still remember the 2004 Indian Ocean earthquake as one of the deadliest in recorded history, and it had a profound impact on the nation.

To honor the memory of those who perished in the 2011 Maldives Tsunami, the nation erected a monument in Male. On the western side of the island, in a little park next to the port, you may find it.

Standing in a circle, the 108 metal rods represent the number of lives lost when the waves crashed into the islands. There was apprehension that the whole nation would be swamped and rendered inhabitable soon after the earthquake. Although this did not materialize, it is a concern that the Maldives may face in the future as a result of increasing sea levels.

It is fitting to pay your respects and get a better understanding of a pivotal moment in history by visiting the Tsunami Monument. Don't let this deter you from visiting the area; earthquakes are common but seldom generate tsunamis of this magnitude.

Address: Thin Ruh Park, Boduthakurufaanu Magu, Male, Maldives

16. Old Friday Mosque & Islamic Center

You may not realize it at your resort, but Islam is very much a part of Maldives culture in the city and on the islands. The Old Friday Mosque and the Islamic Center, which is next to it, are two of Male's most popular attractions.

Regardless of one's religious beliefs, the Old Friday Mosque is a stunning architectural gem and a priceless artifact from the Maldives' ancient past. One of the first mosques in the nation and Southeast Asia, it dates back to the mid-1600s. Crafted from a particular kind of coral rock—a plentiful and durable construction material on the islands—it stands tall and proud in the middle of the city.

There are few places as well-known as the Islamic Center in all of Male. Impressive architectural details, such as the building's elaborate woodwork and massive, golden dome roof, have made it famous. There is an Islamic library and a huge conference room within the center, where formal gatherings take place.

The Muliaage Palace and Sultan Park, two additional prominent male landmarks, are conveniently located only a block away from each of these attractions. Travelers are expected to dress modestly in most areas around islands that are not resorts, particularly in close proximity to Islamic shrines.

Address: 5GH6+4W9, Lonuziyaarai Magu, Malé, Maldives

CHAPTER TWO

9 BEST MALDIVES FESTIVALS NOT TO MISS IN 2024

The bulk of the Maldives' festivals have an Islamic theme, reflecting the country's mostly Muslim population. The Maldives celebrate their religious holidays most fervently during Ramadan and Eid.

1. Ramadan

Muslims throughout the world spend the holy month of Ramadan—a time of fasting, prayer, contemplation, and charity—during the ninth month of the Islamic or Lunar calendar. It is claimed that the first lines of the Quran were revealed to the Prophet Muhammad during the latter third of Ramadan, making this portion of the holy month even more fortunate.

The Maldives' government offices are only open from 9 am to 1:30 pm since the bulk of the population is Muslim. There are a lot of private offices that close at 3 o'clock in the afternoon. On the other hand, the holy month has no impact on hotels and resorts. As a matter of fact, this is a great time to go to the Maldives since you can sample several traditional dishes that are only served during this festival. Iftar (the evening meal for breaking the fast) is available at several places. Indulge in some unique rose, apricot, or kamardine-flavored Ramadan drinks. Cultural events such as musical performances, belly dances, and fire dances are also part of the festival.

2. Eid-Ul Fitr

On the first day of the Islamic calendar month of Shawwal, which is the tenth month, is celebrated Eid-ul Fitr, often called Kuda Eid. It signifies the conclusion of Ramadan. The Maldives celebrate the Islamic holy day of Eid-ul Fitr with considerable fervour. Where the new moon is located, it is called Kuda Eid.

Typically, Maldivians gather with loved ones to commemorate the occasion. Giving alms (fitr zakath) to the poor and needy is a major part of this Eid celebration. The festival begins with morning prayer and continues with a discourse in the mosque. Afterwards, they have dinner with friends and family. People participate in traditional festive games and the festivities continue for three days straight. One of the most tranquil traditional festivities in the Maldives is coming up soon; when will you be able to attend?

3. Bodu Eid

On Eid, after the day of Hajj, people celebrate Eid ul Adha. Its relevance stems from the significance of the Hajj, an annual Islamic pilgrimage to Mecca, the holy city. Every Muslim is obligated to perform this religious act once throughout their lifetime.

Because several Maldivian islands practice the Bodu Mas custom on Eid ul Adha, the festival is also known as Bodu Eid. Bodu places enormous stress on the significance of this Eid. In the midst of the islanders' Bodu Mas festival, a large fish fashioned from palm leaves is caught by the fisherman. An old legend states that a gigantic fish called Modu and his companions, the Maali, emerged from the depths of the ocean to start this custom. With the assistance of a holy man, the people finally succeeded in catching the fish after a hard fight. Maali neshun, a kind of dance done by a group of individuals costumed as ghosts, is also an integral part of the festival for this reason.

4. Eid-Ul-Adha

The Islamic festival of Eid-ul-Adha takes place on the tenth day of the twelveth and last month of the lunar calendar, Zul-Hajj or Zil-Hajj. The feast of sacrifice is celebrated on this occasion, which is also called Eid al-Adha. To commemorate Ibrahim's readiness to give up his son Ishmael to Allah, we celebrate this festival.

The sacrifice of an animal to Allah is crucial to this event because it provides meat for the feast and the distribution of food to the needy. Morning prayer, gift exchange, social gatherings to celebrate Eid-ul-Adha, etc., are all customary, as they are in every nation. However, the Maldives also have their own distinct festival traditions, such as street carnivals, where locals dress brightly and participate in musical performances and other cultural activities. The native Maldivian game of bai bala is also the basis for other sporting events. Is one of the Maldives' cultural events something you're prepared to see?

5. Prophet's Birthday

In Islam, the birthday of the prophet Muhammad, who is also known as Mawlid (Mawlid un-Nabi), is honored. According to the lunar calendar, it takes place in the third month of Rabee-ul-Awwal. On the twelfth day, Sunni Muslims observe it, whereas Shia Muslims mark it on the seventeenth day.

As part of the carnival-style celebrations of Mawlid, the mosque is decorated and a huge street parade is held. Reciting well-known Sufi poetry is a way for intellectuals and artists to show their devotion to the Prophet. At the communal meetings, stories about Muhammad's life are often recounted. Giving to the less fortunate, both monetarily and in the form of food donations, rounds off the day. If you want to see one of the most spectacular and well-known festivals in the Maldives, this is definitely the one for you.

6. The Day Maldives Embraced Islam

A celebration of religious harmony, The Day the Maldives Embraced Islam, is observed on the first of Rabi al-Thani, the fourth month of the Islamic calendar. The last Buddhist Maldivian ruler became a Muslim and became known as a Sultan in the 12th century. The Maldives once adhered mostly to Buddhism, but when their monarch converted to Islam, the nation officially adopted Islam. The Maldives officially adopted Islam on this day. Lectures, talks, and religious rites commemorating the history of Muslims converting to Christianity are part of the festivities.

Although one intriguing account is that he converted so that commercial links with Arabian countries may increase, there are several other plausible explanations. Legend has it that once a month, a sea demon named Rannamaari would rise from the water and threaten to wipe out the hamlet unless a virgin girl was sacrificed. As a result, young females in the community were often sacrificed. However, Yousef Shamsuddin-al Tabrizi, an Islamic pilgrim, waited for the demon while dressed as a female. As he waited, he sang Quranic verses, which sent the monster scurrying away.

The Maldives' national festivals, like those of other formerly colonial nations, commemorate the liberation and fight for independence. Over the course of many decades, the Sultanate, Portugal, the Dutch, and finally the British all had sway over the Maldives. Because of this, they have good reason to celebrate the liberation fight, independence, and subsequent substantial advancements.

7. Independence Day Of Maldives

Independence Day is celebrated in the Maldives on July 26th. As part of the festivities, the National Cadet Corps and the National Security Services put on parades. Students from local schools also put up shows.

The Maldives were formerly a British colony, but in 1887 they were elevated to the position of British Protectorate, allowing them more autonomy in their government. However, the British continued to exert control over international affairs, and in exchange, they were to provide security. By the end of 1965, the Maldives had achieved full independence. It is worth noting that the Maldives had a population of just 97,743 when Prime Minister Ibrahim Nasir signed the independence deal with the British.

8. National Day

To commemorate the day when a popular uprising forced the colonial Portuguese to leave the island, the Maldives celebrate their National Day, formally called Qaumee Dhuvas. The Maldives were conquered by the Portuguese in 1558 after they assassinated the native monarch. But Muhammad Thakurufaanu and his armies retook Male in 1573, ending Portugal's fifteen-year hegemony. But the British and the Dutch eventually colonized it.

The first day of the third month of the Islamic calendar, Rabee-ul-Awwal, is National Day. The island country celebrates this day with a plethora of parades, speeches, and rituals honoring the military and the flag. Some areas may even have fireworks.

9. Republic Day

On November 11th, the Maldives celebrate Republic Day to remember the end of the lengthy Sultanate rule and the beginning of the republic in 1968. Also, every five years on this day, the Maldives president is chosen. Speeches and parades were among the official celebratory activities that took place around the nation. Republic Day delicacies such as huni hakuru folhi (coconut cake), bodibaiy (a very sweet rice snack), and masroshi (fish-stuffed pancake) are best enjoyed during this period.

Maldives in January

The weather in the Maldives in January is often warm and dry. The likelihood of precipitation is quite low, and the average temperature is about 27 degrees Celsius. It is a great time to go if you want to avoid having your vacation derailed by severe weather since, generally speaking, it is a pretty tranquil season.

Maldives in February

As the warmest and driest month of the year for the Maldives, February brings in a fresh weather mix. Vacations focused on sunbathing are perfect for this month. On the other hand, you should prepare ahead of time since this is the busiest season.

Maldives in March

In many respects, March is just as popular as February when it comes to weather. You may enjoy the beach and water activities to the same extent; it is hot, dry, and peaceful. On the downside, it's often more humid and has fewer daylight hours.

Maldives in April

The month of April marks the beginning of the year's unofficial spring season and is known for its warmer temperatures and more humidity. Rain, in the form of a few brief showers that tend to fall in the afternoon, ushers in the wet season as well. If you'd rather not endure the relentless heat of the sun all vacation long and are okay with the occasional shower, April is a decent month to arrange your trip.

Maldives in May

Assuming May follows an April-like pattern, the start of the monsoon season is predicted to occur in the month's second half. This period of the year is quite similar to the rainy season, except those storms and unexpected, sometimes violent, winds define it. On average, there will be fifteen days of rain during the month, with showers lasting anything from a few minutes to several hours.

Maldives in June

June weather is somewhat ordinary, resembling the latter part of May with fewer rainy days and cooler air and water temperatures. If you're not afraid of the rain but still don't want to spend all your time in your hotel room, then this is the perfect time to come.

Maldives in July

You should expect a little decrease in temperature as you go through the year and into July. During this season, you may look forward to the occasional downpour, which might last up to a day. At this point in the monsoon season, the winds will determine the outcome. Having lots of sunny hours is also possible, of course.

Maldives in August

During August, the nation experiences increasingly strong winds, rain, and humidity as it enters the second peak of the monsoon season. Be on the lookout for weather warnings, whether they be for light rain or more severe storms, since the weather here is notoriously unpredictable.

Maldives in September

According to the Maldives' official annual data, September is the wettest month. There is some good news, though: this is an off-peak month, so airfare will be much cheaper.

Maldives in October

Once September passes, the weather becomes steadier and more predictable, and the rain and humidity levels begin to decline again. Due to the persistently high winds and choppy waves, this time of year is perfect for water sports. Also, the wind and precipitation are at reasonable levels, so you can relax and enjoy the ride.

Maldives in November

The monsoon season ends this month, and the nation enters its warm and dry season. The fact that there are just six hours of daylight each day is one distinctive aspect of this month compared to others.

Maldives in December

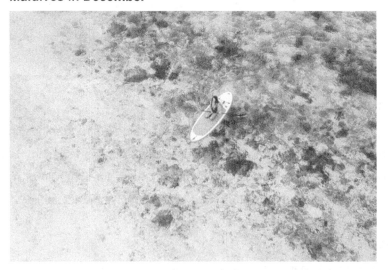

Given the favorable weather, this is a highly sought-after month. The Maldives' official vacation season begins at this point. There is mild, soothing water, plenty of sunshine, and manageable humidity. Then there's the delightful little detail that Christmas is almost here, so you may enjoy your celebration as a vacation.

ESSENTIAL PHRASES TO USE IN MALDIVES FOR TRAVELERS AND TOURISTS

Here's a comprehensive list of essential phrases for travelers and tourists in the Maldives. These phrases will help you communicate effectively and enjoy your time in this beautiful island nation:

Greetings and Basic Phrases:
- Hello - Assalaamu Alaikum
- Good morning - Baajjeveri hendhuneh
- Good afternoon - Baajjeveri madheneh
- Good evening - Baajjeveri fajehraneh
- Good night - Baajjeveri varahba
- Goodbye - Dhanee
- Please - Dhivehiraajje
- Thank you - Shukuriyaa
- Excuse me - Ma-aafu kurey
- Sorry - Ma-aafu kurey
- Yes - Aan
- No - Noon
- Maybe - Haalhiya
- I don't understand - Maafa kurey

Getting Around:
- Where is...? - ... Keevareh?
- How much is this? - Miadhu eh hoadhama?
- Can you help me? - Adhihama kihiney?
- I need a taxi - Taxi kuriah dhenneh
- How far is it? - Kihaa hurihaa?
- Is it near? - Baajjeveri miadhu?

Accommodation:

- Hotel - Hulhule' gai
- Room - Koshi
- Reservation - Huneh kuranee
- Check-in - Dhuniye kihiney
- Check-out - Dhuniye nikuneh
- Can I have the bill, please? - Faahaga ekani, dhanyavaadu
- Wi-Fi password - Wi-Fi password?

Food and Dining:

- Restaurant - Mas Huni Raa
- Menu - Menyu
- Water - Ubu
- Breakfast - Haaluun hedhuneh
- Lunch - Dhooni
- Dinner - Rathee
- Vegetarian - Gulhun
- I am allergic to... - ... Ga allergy eh

Shopping:

- How much does this cost? - Miadhu eh hoadhama?
- Can I have a discount? - Dheysheehi haa bolhuva?
- I would like to buy this - Miadhu ekani haalu kurumeh
- Do you accept credit cards? - Credit cardu thaneh kihiney?

Emergency:

- Help! - Magey ufulu kurumeh!

- I need a doctor - Vaidhu kurey
- Where is the hospital? - Asadhun kihiney?
- Police - Fandiyaaruge
- I lost my passport - Passporuge therikurey
- Leisure and Activities:
- Beach - Fulhadhoo
- Snorkeling - Dheebajaanu
- Scuba diving - Bajanu
- Excursion - Holhuashi
- Sunset - Fannu
- Sunrise - Hen'dhuneh fannu

Numbers:

- 1 - Eku
- 2 - Dhen
- 3 - Thihthi
- 4 - Haadhi
- 5 - Fahthi
- 6 - Haah
- 7 - Huleh
- 8 - Maah
- 9 - Nuva
- 10 - Dhaa

Time and Dates:

- What time is it? - Kihiney gadi?
- Today - Inthihaaru
- Tomorrow - Miyadhu

- Yesterday - Neiy
- Week - Huvaas
- Month - Maas
- Year - Boahun

Expressing Likes and Dislikes:
- I like it - Adhives magey miadhu
- I don't like it - Adhives magey miadhu noon
- It's beautiful - Saafu miadhu
- It's too hot - Ehun balaeh miadhu
- It's too cold - Hithan balaeh miadhu

Weather:
- What's the weather like today? - Inthihaaru kihaa heevaage?
- It's sunny - Fahu miadhu
- It's raining - Maagu miadhu
- It's windy - Baarah miadhu
- It's cloudy - Mehun miadhu

Common Expressions:
- I love Maldives - Maldives ge therein
- Beautiful - Saafu
- Wonderful - Aashaa
- Amazing - Lavaahumeh
- I'm happy - Bajjehee
- I'm sad - Baajjehi

Congratulations - Ufaaveri hukumeh

Cultural Etiquette:

- Can I take a photo? - Rasmee hathaleynu miadhu?
- Is there a dress code? - Libaasee hukumeh?
- May I visit the mosque? - Masjiduge namatheejeh?

Transportation:

- Bus - Bus
- Boat - Dhoni
- Airport - Furamadhu
- Port - Bandharu
- Taxi - Taxi
- Where is the bus stop? - Bus stop kihaa hedhey?

Health and Well-being:

- I need a pharmacy - Pharmacy kurey
- I'm not feeling well - Haalu kihiney
- Can you recommend a good doctor? - Baajjeveri vaidhueh kihiney?

General Inquiries:

- What is your name? - Adhives hedhumeh?
- Where are you from? - Hihvaru kihaa hedhey?
- How long have you been here? - Kihaa hedhumeh therein?
- Can you help me with directions? - Raajjeyge dhoniya kihiney?

Social Interactions:

- May I join you? - Edhige dhanee?

- What's your favorite Maldivian dish? - Maldives miadhu hedhuneh miadhu miadhu kiyaafa?
- Can we be friends? - Mithibee kihiney?

Remember to adapt these phrases to your specific situation and enjoy your time in the Maldives.

CHAPTER THREE

PACKING LIST: THE ULTIMATE MALDIVES PACKING LIST FOR WOMEN & MEN

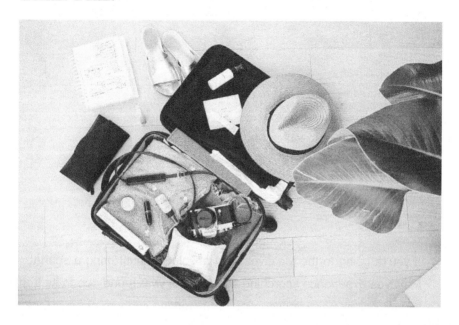

You must take the weather and your intended activities into account when you prepare for the Maldives. Sunglasses and other items to block the sun and sand should also be brought along. Sunburn and backaches are the last things you want, after all, to spoil the fun.

If you're planning a trip to the Maldives, these are the items of apparel and accessories that I think are essential.

Sunhat

If you're going to the Maldives, you absolutely must bring a sunhat. The Maldives experience scorching sunshine all year round due to its tropical location. Sunscreen is essential for preventing sunburn on your face and neck.

For the best protection, bring a wide-brimmed sun hat. To further shield your skin from the sun, you might search for hats that provide ultraviolet (UV) protection.

Sandals/Flip-Flops
It's likely that you'll spend a great deal of time outside, strolling the shore. Bring light, breathable shoes that won't add extra pounds to your bag.

I suggest bringing along an extra pair of sandals to go with your evening attire and one for exploring the resort. For your time at the beach, don't forget to bring a pair of flip-flops. Your cute sandals will stay clean and dry in this manner.

Sunglasses

You can't go to the Maldives without sunglasses. Being so close to the equator means that the sun is more intense in the Maldives.

Sunglasses that block ultraviolet light are an essential item to have on hand so that you can avoid straining your eyes from staring at the sun all day. The Maldives are an ideal place to wear polarized sunglasses since they protect eyes from the sun's brightness and UV radiation.

Rain Jacket

A raincoat might be necessary, depending on the time of year you visit. You may wish to pack one in case you go during the wetter months.

Between May and December, the Maldives sees an increase in rainfall due to changes in wind patterns and generally colder air temperatures.

It rained for a few minutes here and there while I was there during the rainy season, but that's okay. It cooled down just enough to be pleasant. Also, don't worry if you forget to bring an umbrella; most resorts provide them. If you plan on riding your bike around the island during the rain, a rain jacket is a good investment.

Swimsuits

Be sure you bring a swimsuit that is suitable for the dress code of your Maldives resort. Your choice of swimwear is likely to be unrestricted (within certain limits, of course) when you book a private island resort. But bring additional cover-ups if you're planning on staying on Male's main island.

You should dress modestly on the mainland of the Maldives because the nation is mostly Muslim. While bikinis are ideal for lounging in the sun, one-piece swimsuits are more practical for water sports like scuba diving and snorkeling.

Swimsuit Coverups

You shouldn't only bring swimwear; additionally, bring some light, comfy coverups to wear while you're not in the water or soaking up some rays.

In particular, I hid my identity when I sprang from the water to get food. It was easy for me to move about, and I didn't even have to go back to my overwater cottage to change.

Sundresses/Rompers

Bring along some rompers and sundresses for your Maldives vacation. Wearing a sundress or romper to the resort for breakfast, lunch, or supper is a great idea. Island hopping and general exploration are two other things they excel at.

Maxi Dress

There will likely be both more sophisticated and more informal dining options at your resort. Dressing formally is expected while dining at high-end restaurants.

Maxi dresses are perfect for this occasion. They are the epitome of sophistication and go well with sandals. The nicest aspect is that you won't have to sacrifice comfort for authenticity.

Shorts

Along with rompers and sundresses, you should also have a pair of shorts on hand.

Whether you're going for a swim, a boat ride, or just a leisurely walk around the resort, shorts are the way to go. Be sure to bring along a pair for pedaling around the resort.

T-Shirts/Tank Tops

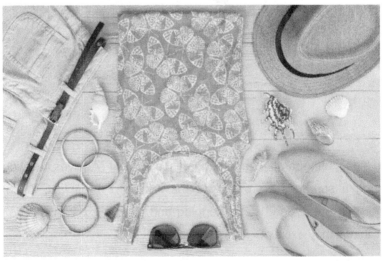

As a tomboy like myself, you may want to round up your Maldives packing list with a few tees and tank tops. On days when I'm not swimming, my go-to tropical holiday attire consists of shorts and t-shirts.

In addition to keeping, you cool and comfy, they are perfect for all of your scheduled activities. A lovely blouse paired with denim shorts is a pretty and easy outfit option that you may bring along.

Sunscreen
Bringing sunscreen is a must while visiting the Maldives, as it is with any beach vacation.
You should bring sunscreen to the Maldives since, being a tropical country, the temperature is hot and muggy all year round.

Bring sunblock that is safe for reefs. Using sunscreen that isn't reef-safe will put the stunning coral reefs of the Maldives at risk of chemical damage.

In order to return home with skin that seems like it was sun-kissed, be sure to include a sunscreen lotion that contains bronzer. Even on overcast days, the sun's rays may be intense, so it's important to protect yourself by using sunscreen.

Underwater Camera
A high-quality underwater camera is a must-have for exploring the Maldives' beautiful blue seas and capturing the vibrant marine life.

Impressive stills and moving footage may be captured by a number of high-quality underwater cameras, such as the GoPro Hero 10 and the Nikon Coolpix W300 16MP 4K Ultra HD Waterproof Digital Camera.

Dry Bag

You might use the dry bags that are provided by many resorts. You should probably carry one just in case. When you're swimming or snorkeling, a dry bag is the way to keep your devices, including your camera. If you plan on doing boat excursions to the adjacent islands or other beaches, it will be useful as well.

Wet Bag

If your accommodation offers a dry bag, they'll likely also provide a wet bag.

When you're done using an item—like a swimsuit, towel, or anything else drenched in water or sand—a wet bag is the perfect place to keep it. Additionally, it works well for separating your clean and dirty laundry.

Snorkeling Gear

Make sure to inquire about this in advance, since it is something that the majority of high-end resorts provide. If the snorkeling gear isn't supplied, it's recommended that you bring your own so you may explore the marine life and blue waters.

A wide variety of sharks, manta rays, parrotfish, seahorses, dolphins, and many more marine creatures will be visible to you.

Water Bottle

Because staying hydrated is important to most resorts, bottled water is often provided. This is especially true when you're in the midst of the Indian Ocean.

It is recommended to pack a refillable water bottle in order to remain hydrated when visiting nearby islands or while staying in Male.

Travel Insurance

Everyone planning a trip to the Maldives should get travel insurance before they go. Your Maldives vacation is an adventure where you can't predict when you could become sick or hurt. This policy will protect you in the event that your bags go missing or that your flight is delayed.

Because unexpected things may and will happen, make sure to include travel insurance in your Maldives packing list.

Adapter

An adaptor is necessary since the Maldives run on 230 volts. You may inquire or check with certain resorts in advance to see if they give one, but it's more convenient to carry your own.

Beach Bag

On your way to or from the beach, you may throw in your sunscreen, hat, and sunglasses. If the one they supply isn't to your liking or if you already possess a fashionable one, you are welcome to bring your own.

Cash

You may not think to bring cash with you to the Maldives, but you should.

Medication

Bring any necessary medications for your Maldives holiday, just in case. It's better to be proactive than reactive. Always have the original prescription(s) on hand in case customs officials request them while traveling with medicine.

Medical Kit

While a full medical kit isn't necessary, it is wise to have bandages and gauze on hand. Staying on a private island might force you to go to the main island in the event of an emergency.

Until you can receive medical help, you may use some of the items in your first aid kit. When swimming or just relaxing on the beach, it's impossible to predict when someone will suffer a jellyfish sting or any other kind of harm.

Insect Repellent

Mosquitoes are a common problem in the Maldives Islands due to the abundance of vegetation. Since it is unpleasant to get bit by mosquitoes while trying to relax, you should bring insect repellent.

Passport

If you're planning a trip to the Maldives, your passport is an absolute must-have. I don't know why so many individuals get so thrilled about packing their clothing and other essentials that they forget to bring their passports. It's baffling, really.

Verify that your passport is current and has a validity date of at least six months.

CHAPTER FOUR

GETTING AROUND IN MALDIVES- A GUIDE FOR GETTING AROUND IN THE CITY

Every island in the Maldives, whether it's a public or private resort, is small enough to easily explore on foot. This is why the Maldives do not have any automobile rental agencies, yet the larger islands do have taxis. Walking around an island is the best and most economical way to see what it has to offer. You have a few solid choices when it comes to getting from one island to another.

94

Air Travel

Air travel is the main way that most tourists get to and around the Maldives. Located on Hulhulé Island, close to Malé, the capital city, Velana International Airport serves as the primary point of entry for the nation. A lot of internal flights to the other inhabited islands go through it, and it's also a hub for a lot of foreign carriers.

A strong domestic aviation network is essential due to the geographical dispersion of the Maldives. The national airline, Maldivian, operates regular flights to more than a dozen domestic airports, providing connections to various regions of the nation. Seaplanes and other tiny propeller aircraft often do domestic trips, allowing passengers to take in breathtaking vistas as they travel between islands.

Speedboat

Tourists often use speedboats as their means of inter-island transit after landing at either the major or a smaller airport. The speedboat is an alternative to using a ferry for those who either do not want to or are unable to do so. You have the option to arrange for your own speedboat transportation or have the resort do it for you. Depending on the resort and the distance to be traveled, the costs may reach as high as MVR 3,500, which is rather costly.

Ferry

Taking a ferry across the water between islands is a more economical choice. The Maldives Transport and Contracting Company (MTCC) operates the public ferries that connect the inhabited islands. Although slower than speedboats, ferries are a great way to get around town, especially for those on a tighter budget. They also give you a chance to meet islanders and see how they live their everyday lives. For a trip that lasts more than five hours, prices range from thirty to sixty million Vietnamese dong. The cost of a private ferry from the airport to Male is around MVR 40, but the cost of a public boat between islands is roughly MVR 30-75. From six in the morning to six in the afternoon, you may find the majority of them. Despite being the most cost-effective alternative, there are a few drawbacks to these ferries that may cause you to rethink your decision. You can't rely on ferries since they are often late. The resort islands are not served by the boats, and they are not even operational on Fridays.

Seaplane

If you're in a rush, a seaplane is your best bet; in no more than 90 minutes, you may be dropped off at the farthest resorts from Male or vice versa. In addition, the low-flying heights of these aircraft provide stunning aerial views of the islands and reefs. Those unspoiled, deserted islands will also be visible to you. There are a few drawbacks, however, such as the fact that these seaplanes don't fly at night and the possibility that your bags may have to go separately. Prices start at 3,500 MVR and go up to 7,000 MVR. However, if your budget permits, you must not miss out on this one-of-a-kind opportunity.

Maldivian 'Dhoni'

Dhonis, the traditional wooden boats of the Maldives, have played a crucial role in the archipelago's transportation network for many years. The classic Arab sailing vessel known as a dhow is very similar to a Dhoni. They have a function in the tourist sector in addition to their traditional uses in fishing and transporting goods. You may go on sunset cruises or trips to nearby islands on Dhonis, which are offered by several resorts. You may find a number of Dhonis waiting in the harbor at the airport ferry pier; just follow the coastline all the way to the eastern end of Boduthakurufaanu Magu. The daily rate might be anything from 1,000 to 1,500 MVR. An idyllic Dhoni boat across the Maldives at twilight is the icing on the cake for a honeymoon couple.

Yacht

A yacht is the most luxurious means of local transportation in the Maldives for the well-heeled, as it can take you to secluded islands and reefs. While you're here, you may rent a boat and enjoy the open sea in style and luxury. Your broker can create an ideal schedule for your party, whether you bring your own boat or hire a private charter. The yacht's size, the amenities offered, and other factors determine the rates. On a daily basis, a crewed motor boat with three cabins could accommodate six guests for around 55,000 MVR.

Bus

The Maldives Transport and Contracting Company (MTCC) runs bus service, which is a more affordable alternative; however, it only goes on certain routes. Commuter bus prices between Male and Hulhulmale begin at MVR 3. Passengers arriving at any of the Maldives' airports may take a shuttle bus to Hulhulmale for MVR 20. The bus stop is conveniently located only 50 meters from the airport exit. The timing is highly dependent on the quantity of traffic; thus, the frequency of every half hour is just an estimate. Avoid getting on the bus if you're carrying a lot of bags, and be prepared for the buses to be packed during the wet seasons.

Cycle

Picture this: you're riding a bike in a peaceful setting on flat routes dotted with the shadows of coconut trees, taking in fresh air and enjoying a gentle breeze. It sounds fantastic, doesn't it? Of course! If you want to see the major islands, this is a great option. Resorts such as Senova Fushi, Island Hideaway, Diva, Shangri-La, etc. provide bikes and other transportation options for guests, even if rental services are not yet accessible. Guests of the Shangri-La Villingili Resort may take advantage of guided bike trips that round the atoll. If you're a lover of cycling and your hotel doesn't supply one, you may always bring a foldable bike with you.

Taxi

There is an effective taxi service in cities where driving is common, such as Male and Addu. From the airport to your destination, it is fairly easy to hail a taxi in Male. The trip will be pleasant and air-conditioned. After 11:00 PM, the fare jumps to MVR 30, but before that, it's about MVR 20 for any distance. Carrying bags could result in an additional MVR 10 fee for trunk use. Just because the facility is tiny doesn't mean you should be worried if a cab drops by to pick you up and is already carrying other passengers. A taxi may be readily ordered via your hotel or guesthouse, or you can utilize a service like Dialacab, Loyal Taxi, or New Taxi.

Here are the many modes of transportation available in the Maldives; now it's up to you to choose the one that works best for you to ensure a pleasant journey.

BEST PLACE TO SHOP IN MALDIVES
Male Local Market

As you step foot in Male Local Market, the Maldives' shopping experience takes a thrilling turn. This massive marketplace, situated on the northern shoreline, is among the most visited street markets in the Maldives. This bazaar is popular among residents and visitors alike because of the wide variety of local arts and crafts, souvenirs, and gift goods sold at its many booths. The standout features of these markets are the kiosks that offer regional foods.

Hours of operation: 8:00 am to 11:00 pm

Location: Male' Higun, Maldives

Majeedhee Magu

The massive Maldives street market, Majedhee Magu, is located right in the middle of town. Everything you could possibly want, from clothing to accessories to technology, is at your fingertips. When you're shopping in the Maldives, don't be afraid to haggle over prices. Indulge in mouthwatering Maldivian food at one of the many fantastic restaurants, such as Caf-Asia.

Hours of operation: 9:00 am to 11:00 pm

Address: Majedhee Magu Road, Male, Maldives

Le Cute

Stop by Le Cute, a famous Maldives retail beauty store, if you're a fan of cosmetics and fragrances. The finest things to buy in the Maldives may be found at this posh store, which deals with cosmetics, toiletries, health care items, and herbal remedies.

When to visit: 9:30 am to 11:00 pm, 4:00 pm to 6:00 pm & 8 Pm to 1:00 pm on Fridays
Address: Majedhee Magu Road, Male, Maldives

STO Trade Centre

An authentic Maldivian shopping experience is offered at STO Trade Centre. The home goods department is on the first floor, while the souvenir counters are on the second and third floors. The STO Trade Centre is one of the greatest shopping destinations in the Maldives, and it sees a steady stream of customers from all over the world.

Hours of operation: 8:30 am to 10:00 pm
Address: Orchid Magu, Male, Maldives

Island Bazaar

Shopping at Island Bazaar will never be the same since this premium store showcases the elaborate handicrafts of local artists in addition to selling fashionable lifestyle items. Beautiful and unique patterns adorn every item, from cushions to shoulder bags to handcrafted fridge magnets. For those Maldivian shoppers in search of a one-of-a-kind, exquisite present, this is a top destination.

Hours of operation: 10:00 am to 6:00 pm and 4:00 pm to 6:00 pm on Fridays:

Address: M.Karishma, Level 1, Fareedhee Magu, Male', Maldives

Centro Mall

Make your way to Centro Mall in Hulhumale if you're in the market for high-end retailers, trendy restaurants, and entertainment areas. It is without a doubt the poshest spot in the Maldives for high-end retail therapy, with over 30 brand outlets and flagship shops, posh salons and spas, and posh restaurants like Manhattan Fish Market.

Hours of operation: 7:00 am to 12:00 pm

Address: Hulhumale, Maldives

Chaandhanee Magu

Chaandhanee Magu is one of the most well-known retail centers in the Maldives. Here you may discover remarkable selections of both local and international items, in addition to handicrafts. Singapore Bazaar is a common name for Chaandhanee Magu among locals since Singapore is a major supplier of imported items.

Hours of operation: 9:00 am to 11:00 pm
Address: North Male Atoll, Maldives

Nala Boutique

Discover the exquisite collection of designer clothing and accessories at Nala Boutique. One of the most well-known boutiques in the Maldives, this one is located inside the Kurumba Maldives Resort. There is a wide variety of clothing and accessories for ladies, as well as beach toys and children's dresses, at this store.

Hours of operation: 8:30 am to 10:00 pm
Address: Kurumba Maldives, Vihamanafushi, North Male Atoll Maldives

Angolo Souvenir Shop

The Angolo Souvenir Shop is often regarded as the finest among the several Maldives souvenir shops. This charming tiny boutique on Maafushi Island, just off the coast of Mahe, sells a wide variety of creative and eccentric items that pay homage to Maldivian culture. The proprietors are also very kind and helpful. When you purchase a memento from this store, they even offer you a taste of their banana coconut. The nicest part of visiting Maafushi, Maldives, is shopping for unique and reasonably priced items, such as tea, bags, shirts, refrigerator magnets, and keychains.

Hours of operation: 10 am to 9 pm
Address: Maafushi, South Male Atoll, Valu Magu, H 29548, Maldives

Oevaali Art Shop
In 2015, sisters Raniya and Raya Mansoor established the Oevaali Art Shop with the goal of introducing everyone to Maldivian history and culture through visual arts and design. You may find a wide variety of

Maldives souvenirs, including paintings, sculptures, and more, in the art and souvenir store. You can trust that everything you buy at the Oevaali Art Shop is authentically Maldivian, and the store is known as a leading brand in the local art and culture scene. Art and crafts from this establishment are worth every cent and make great gifts for friends and family; however, they are a little pricey due to their popularity, quality, and long history.

Hours of operation: 10 am to 6 pm
Address: H. Gaathu Giri, Bodufungandu Magu, Male 20008

Male International Airport

After you get through airport customs and immigration, it's time to start shopping. Stop by the duty-free area at Male International Airport—it's got every sort of retailer imaginable. When you're in the Maldives, you must visit this incredible mall. You may conduct some last-minute shopping at the airport if you happen to have neglected to get anything for your loved ones. The majority of tourists do that.

Address: Airport Main Rd, 22000, Maldives

Resort Shop

Your Maldives resort probably has a gift shop where you can pick up some souvenirs to remember your time there. Prices at these establishments might be very steep. But really, who are you going to stop if you have the cash? When you're stuck on an island in the Maldives and there aren't any nearby shopping malls, these resort stores are a lifesaver. Stop hesitating and just purchase it if something good catches your attention.

Hours of operation: 9:00 am to 11:00 pm

Address: Maldives

10 BEST THINGS TO BUY IN MALDIVES

Numerous established and up-and-coming businesses have set up shop in the Maldives to meet the needs of the numerous tourists that come to this island country to do their shopping. Curious about the Maldives' most popular items? Some of the greatest Maldivian souvenirs are these.

1. Thumdu Kuna

In case you were wondering, Thumbu Kunaa are traditional Maldivian mats. The women of the islands start with natural fibers and weave them after that. They are the most unique and creative souvenirs to purchase in the Maldives because of the geometric designs and many forms they come in. Alternatively, you could purchase the ones with golden laces that ancient rulers wore. Although the native Maldivians used them for sleeping and worshiping, you may now utilize them as beautiful decorative pieces in your house.

Where to buy: Chaandhanee Magu

2. Lacquer Products

Among the many traditional Maldivian handicrafts, lacquer work is a must-buy for anybody wishing to bring a little bit of the country's rich history back home. A wide variety of exquisitely carved lacquer goods, including vases, boxes, plates, baskets, toys, and pens, are available for purchase. These items are a sight to see in the local marketplaces of the Maldives. They are brightly colored with various lasting paints in shades of red, yellow, and black, which are specifically extracted from the juice of a certain tree. Sultan Park in the Maldives is a great place to take the kids for a leisurely stroll after a day of shopping.

Where to buy: Chaandhanee Magu

3. **Dhonis**

Yes, we are referring to the smaller dhonis that are used for sailing in the Maldives when we say that the traditional boats are among the most remarkable items to purchase in the country. As a memento of your time in the Maldives, you may pick up one of the many charming and intricate miniatures sold in the many art and souvenir stores across the nation. Traditional Maldivian fishing boats crafted from wood and adorned with sails are a popular attraction for sightseers because of their attractive design and intricate craftsmanship.

Where to buy: Majeedhee Magu, Husnuheenaa Magu, Chaandhanee Magu

4. **Maldivian Sarongs**

You can't leave the Maldives without purchasing one, or more, of the brightly colored sarongs sold in the local marketplaces and bazaars if you're in the market for beachwear. This stunning seaside town is a great location to get trendy sarongs in bright colors and charming flower motifs. You may wear a Maldivian sarong to a variety of events, from beach parties to barbecues, thanks to the wide variety of colors and designs available. It will undoubtedly serve as an aesthetically pleasing addition to your shopping bags, evoking jealousy among your pals back home! February is the perfect time to wear one if you're visiting the Maldives.

Where to buy: Majeedhee Magu

5. **Coconut Items**

Not only is the Maldives a popular beach destination, but the abundance of coconuts here allows locals to produce a wide variety of attractive handicrafts and strange practical goods, making coconut products among the most sought-after souvenirs from the country. The remaining portion of this huge fruit is kept even after the pulp has been eaten. Coconuts are used in many different industrial contexts, including but not limited to their outer crust, bark, leaves, and stems. Various boutiques and souvenir shops in the Maldives sell a wide range of objects made from coconut palm wood, shells, and leaves. These include sculptures, vases, wall hangings, baskets, bowls, spatulas, lampshades, coir ropes, mats, bags, and much more.

Where to buy: Male Market, Maafushi Island, STO Trade Centre

6. Traditional Jewelry

Since the Maldives is a shopping paradise, women seldom have to think about what to buy while there. Here you may find a wide variety of goods, including clothing, headwear, sarongs, organic cosmetics, and exquisite Maldivian jewelry. It's true, women! You may find a wide selection of unique and inexpensive souvenirs in any of Male's flea markets or street bazaars. These include necklaces, bracelets, and earrings crafted from seashells, coconut fiber, stones, earthenware, tree raisins, and seeds, among other natural materials. Pearl jewelry is also available here; however, it could be a little pricey.

Where to buy: Male, Fareedhee Magu's Island Bazaar, Majeedhee Magu

7. Organic Cosmetics

Those who want to utilize natural cosmetics to maintain youthful, radiant skin for as long as possible can also find what they're looking for in the Maldives. It is common knowledge that hair oils, body oils, moisturizers, and culinary oils are all made from virgin coconut oil because of its abundance of nutrients. Believe it or not, the Maldives is one of the most advanced tropical countries that has figured out how to use coconut oil. The Maldives has perfected the art of guest pampering with its array of organic cosmetic products created here from coconuts. Renowned Maldivian companies like Kaashi Theyo, Frella, and Faan provide a variety of items that promise high-quality outcomes at affordable prices.

Where to buy: Kaashi Theyo (Malé), Frella (Malé), and Faan

8. Packaged Fish Products

You would wish you could bring some seafood home after indulging in the mouth-watering dishes served in Maldives eateries. And you know what? Of course, you can! Travelers visiting the Maldives may actually buy fish items in packaging that they can eat within three to four days.

Bring some of the delicious Maldivian food to your friends and family by picking up some vacuum-packed or canned fish filets, smoked fish, chipped dry fish, or fish pickles from this store.

Where to buy: Majeedhee Magu and Male

9. Fridge Magnets

Fridge magnets are a safe bet if you're shopping in the Maldives for a gift for someone's fridge. In the Maldives, you may find a wide variety of unique fridge magnets at any number of stores and marketplaces. You can bring a touch of the tropics into your house by hanging them on your refrigerator. A tropical Maldives bridge will be on your mind every time you reach for a beer can in the fridge.

Where to buy: Majeedhee Magu, Husnuheenaa Magu, Chaandhanee Magu

10. Wicker Mats

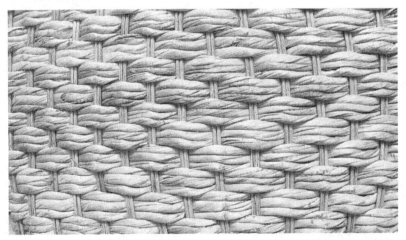

While shopping in the Maldives, you should definitely check out the wicker mats. You can't go wrong with these handcrafted items as mementos of your tropical island vacation. You won't be able to help but purchase these items for your house because of how lovely they are. These mats will add style to your room and spark interesting conversations.

Where to buy: Majeedhee Magu, Husnuheenaa Magu, Chaandhanee Magu

CHAPTER FIVE

WHERE TO STAY IN MALDIVES: BEST AREAS & NEIGHBORHOODS
TO VISIT IN MALDIVES

Amilla Fushi

Since its launch in 2016, Amilla Fushi has sprinted into the top tier of Maldives luxury resorts, bringing with it a fresh and exciting vibe reminiscent of Miami Beach. Amilla Fushi has quickly become a popular spot for the well-heeled younger set, thanks to its 54-glistening white contemporary water villas, 8 opulent beach homes, and 5 one-of-a-kind treehouses. Each of these accommodations has effortlessly chic interior design and, in the majority of instances, enormous private pools. Along with its picture-perfect beach and massive infinity pool, it has a selection of high-end restaurants that can satisfy even the pickiest eater.

Gili Lankanfushi

Gili Lankanfushi is only a ten-minute speedboat ride from Male Airport, but the island's no-shoes, no-news mentality, and forty-five magnificent, multi-level wood houses make it seem like a world apart from the rest of the nation. All but the bedrooms are open to the outside in these villas, which have outdoor showers, stairs leading down to the lagoon, and a rooftop terrace perfect for stargazing with a flute of champagne. An attraction in and of itself, the island's restaurants are headed by executive chef Aldo Cadau, who oversees a variety of eateries, one of which is By the Sea, a Japanese fine-dining establishment that unquestionably ranks among the best in the nation.

St Regis Vommuli

Your personal butler will send you a video message to introduce themselves while your chauffeur-driven Bentley takes you to the seaplane terminal at Male Airport. This new resort in Dhaalu Atoll is one of the sexiest and most modern boltholes you'll ever see. The island is mostly undiscovered by tourists. St. Regis stands out with its modern design, magnificent spa, and 77 completely automated villas—where you can anticipate iPad-controlled air-con and digitally triggered blinds—on a lovely, jungle-clad coral island flanked by bright blue seas. The hotel brings its city-hotel sensibility to this stunning location. From little beach cottages with private pools to the grand John Astor Estate, there is a wide range of 33 land villas and 44 over-water ones.

Cheval Blanc Randheli

Although Kate and Will's honeymoon was at Cheval Blanc, the mansion is sure to be a warm welcome for anybody with two grandkids to spare. Cheval Blanc is owned by LVMH, the parent company of Louis Vuitton.

There are forty-five luxurious homes to choose from, each with its own infinity pool, butler, and unbelievable list of amenities. Arrivals by the resort's branded aircraft and a $100 burger are enough to shock even seasoned travelers to the most exclusive hotels in the world.

One & Only Reethi Rah

Quiet opulence has no place here. Utilizing reclaimed ground, One & Only increased the area of an existing island by more than three times and built 130 expensive homes on it. Almost every villa has its own private lap pool and offers breathtaking views of the ocean. Royalty, Hollywood A-listers, and everyone else looking to turn heads by the breathtaking black-slate infinity pool frequent Reethi Rah, which combines Balinese fantasy with a glitterati fashion show.

Soneva Fushi

The first Maldives back-to-nature resort, Soneva Fushi, is hard to think of a finer place for families to vacation. Children under the age of ten will be begging their parents to take them to Soneva Fushi's purpose-built jungle lair every morning since it houses what is perhaps the greatest kids' club in the nation. Kids as young as four won't have a dull moment with two pools, a pirate ship, a movie theater, a dressing room, a Lego play area, and daily activities including culinary workshops, music lessons, and evening astronomy presentations. While their little ones play, parents may unwind on the beautiful island's beaches, swim in their own pools, or dine at one of the six fantastic restaurants tucked away in the lush foliage.

Four Seasons Landaa Giraavaru

Landaa Giraavaru is enormous, standing as it does as a once-thriving coconut grove engulfed in dense forest. With one hundred and thirty-three enormous villas, all of which have sea views or direct beach access, this resort in the Maldives may be the most country club-like of them. In addition to great youth programs for children aged 4 to 12, the marine biology center has fish tanks and a turtle rehabilitation center where damaged turtles are cared for and eventually released back into the water.

Niyama Private Islands

Niyama, which translates to "bon voyage" in the native Divehi language, is really two islands joined by a causeway and separated into "concepts" of relax and play, and it has recently won a slew of accolades for its unique services. Families will love this place because of its welcoming atmosphere; kids may run free virtually anywhere, but they'll especially like the play island. Here you may find the top-notch kids' club, which provides activities such as dolphin-spotting tours, stage performances, and a splash park for youngsters aged 12 months to 12 years. The villas here are contemporary interpretations of tropical island dreams, with large outdoor baths and private plunge pools (some are offered without them for families).

Ozen by Atmosphere at Maadhoo
This is the most luxurious and remarkable of the three new OZEN-branded resorts that have just opened in the Maldives. It introduces the still-relatively-unusual idea of a Maldives luxury all-inclusive. Here is one spot where it is almost impossible to rack up a minibar bill or discover

any extras added to your accommodation, so families looking for an opulent vacation need look no further. A separate beach only for kids is one of the many great features of the superb and free kids' club. South Male Atoll offers a variety of free watersports and island tours that families will love. High ceilings, beachfront locations, and colorful furnishings—many of which include works of local art and craft—decorate the villas.

Kanuhura

Bright, elegant, and remarkably secluded villas, as well as an outstanding array of dining choices, now grace Kanuhura, which reopened last year after a comprehensive and inventive refurbishment. The accommodations here are now defined by curated libraries, indoor-outdoor bathrooms, and private plunge pools, but Kanuhura in Lhaviyani Atoll has been a favorite among travelers for a long time due to the picture-perfect white expanse that runs along the lagoon. Plus, there's a private "picnic island" only a short boat trip away, so you can indulge in all your Robinson Crusoe fancies (with the added bonus of always being close to a refreshing beer and some delicious tuna). Kanuhura is a favorite among families because it contains the Boduberu Lounge, which is reserved exclusively for children, and because it hosts events like animal safaris, pottery lessons, and outdoor movie screenings.

Summer Island

Summer Island is a long-running, cheap resort in the North Male Atoll. In 2015, it underwent a complete refurbishment and emerged dazzling with new rooms, water villas, and trendy public spaces. Beautiful white sand beaches, excellent snorkeling in the lagoon (which recently had the world's first 3D printed reef added to it to supplement the coral growths and provide more habitat for marine life), and a fraction of the price of nearby jetsetter hangouts make Summer Island feel luxurious without breaking the bank. Anyone seeking a laid-back beach vacation, as well as divers who may choose from a multitude of adjacent reefs, like to go there.

Equator Village

This eccentric spot gets its moniker from its position on the southernmost atoll in the Maldives, Addu. Even though most travelers already have a long trip ahead of them due to the hour-long flight from Male, the inexpensive costs and welcoming atmosphere more than make up for it. Equator Village is located in what was once the barracks of the British RAF base and is in stark contrast to the expensive, ostentatious resorts that can be found across the country. Instead, it caters to a more modest demographic by offering simple, inexpensive, and unpretentious entertainment. Since its renovation in 2017, it has become an even more popular option for families and divers looking for an inexpensive vacation.

The Barefoot Eco Hotel

At the country's northernmost tip, you'll find this boutique-yet-affordable guesthouse, which combines the best of both worlds: the low prices and plenty of local flavor of a guesthouse with the advantages of life on a private island (immaculate empty beaches, glamorous and beautifully designed rooms). The resort is set in lush tropical vegetation and has a stunning white coral sand beach bordered by azure seas. If it weren't for the alcohol ban, it would be impossible to say you're on a native island.

Angsana Velavaru

If you value a nice location to reside but are wary about taking out a second mortgage, Angsana is a reasonably priced alternative to consider. Villas here are great without pillow menus or personal butlers, but they still have outdoor baths, private pools, and access to the beach or sea. Many also include espresso machines and other conveniences.

The In-Ocean Residences, which are well-liked by couples looking for a romantic getaway, are located on water in the lagoon and are only accessible by boat from the main island. The island's beautiful beaches also deserve special mention.

Shamar Guesthouse & Dive

On the "local" (i.e., Maldivian) island of Maamigili, you'll find this charming hotel, perfect for a budget-friendly diving vacation. It's the antithesis of a resort—a very unpretentious and welcoming spot with sand floors in the common rooms and an overall village atmosphere. Smack dab in the midst of a Maldivian island, where the residents are sure to be kind and where you may hear the call to prayer five times a day. Naturally, this implies that you won't be able to get any alcoholic beverages on the island. However, there are two diving boats that leave every day, and you have a good chance of seeing whale sharks, which swim in these waters all year.

Shangri-La Villingili Resort & Spa

Shangri-La, located in the country's far south, is another resort that needs an additional hour or two of travel time to get there. However, the sheer magnitude of what awaits you at the resort more than justifies the trip. A nine-hole golf course, tennis courts, a complete gym and spa, yoga, Pilates, and activities like traditional Maldivian night fishing are all part of Shangri-La, one of the largest luxury resort islands in the nation. Even the highest point in the nation, a grassy knoll 5 meters tall, is located on this relatively large island. It also has three freshwater lakes that are home to a diverse birdlife. Private pools or steps into the lagoon, beautiful Asian-inspired décor, and really luxurious bathrooms are just a few of the amenities offered by these large water villas, which also have high ceilings and an incredibly smooth vibe.

CHAPTER SIX

BEST LUXURY HOTELS IN MALDIVES

Waldorf Astoria, Maldives, Ithaafushi

Waldorf Astoria Maldives Ithaafushi was named the best resort hotel in Asia and the third best in the world in the recent announcement of the results of Travel + Leisure's 2022 World's Best Awards.

Guests at the Waldorf Astoria Maldives Ithaafushi resort may enjoy a picturesque setting on a secluded island with crystal-clear waters and stunning sandy beaches, about 45 minutes by boat from Velana International Airport. An exclusive private island, a world-class spa retreat, the first aqua wellness center in the Maldives, and eleven acclaimed dining venues—including Zuma Maldives and Terra—are all part of the resort. The eating pods are made of hand-crafted bamboo.

Guests of all ages may enjoy these and many more activities while at the resort. The Waldorf Astoria Maldives Ithaafushi has an island as well as

119 pool villas on the beach, reef, or in the middle of the ocean. With these rooms plus the rest of the resort's first-rate facilities, you're sure to have an experience like no other.

Spanning 32,000 square meters in the heart of the Indian Ocean, Ithaafushi—The Private Island—is the biggest private island in the Maldives. It is the perfect place to celebrate special occasions with friends and family or to deepen relationships with loved ones, since it can host up to 24 people in two beautifully appointed villas and one four-bedroom house.

Anantara Kihavah Villas, Maldives

The Anantara Kihavah Maldives, a luxury resort island with powdery white dunes and a reputation as the most Instagrammable hotel in the world, offers the height of opulence.

The five-star Anantara Kihavah Maldives resort, situated on the UNESCO Biosphere Reserve of Baa Atoll, encourages you to envision your very own barefoot paradise. Indulge in the peaceful solitude of your own beachfront or overwater home with a private pool. Observe Hawksbill Sea turtles and manta rays while snorkeling. Stargaze until the moon rises. This magical haven is perfect for a romantic dinner on a secluded beach or even underwater. The over-water spa provides world-class treatments that will help you relax even more; these treatments are designed with the medicinal powers of local fruits and plants in mind.

Their Sea, Fire, Space, and Sky four-in-one eating concept is sure to satisfy your cravings. At SEA, an underwater restaurant and wine cellar that has won many awards, you can enjoy modern European dishes paired with fine wines. At Sky, you may toast to blazing sunsets and a starry sky as FIRE and SPICE offer traditional delicacies against open kitchen backgrounds, meters above sea level. Manzaru and Plates are two beachside restaurants that provide breathtaking views of the ocean in a picturesque setting.

Cocoon Maldives

The villas have been designed with the utmost care to guarantee that your stay will be one of unparalleled tranquility. With its own garden, swimming pool, sun loungers, day bed, and outdoor shower, this property is perfect for spending sunny days, and the terrace overlooking the ocean gives a stunning view of the shimmering waves.

The most state-of-the-art Italian architecture blends flawlessly with the breathtaking Maldives scenery, resulting in an exquisite union of nature and architecture. An award-winning Italian designer named LAGO designed each of the 150 guest villas, three restaurants, and two bars at Cocoon.

As the main dining facility of the hotel, the OCTOPUS Restaurant offers a themed buffet with interactive live stations. Couples seeking a romantic evening supper by candlelight as the lovers' moon rises may choose the à la carte menu at the lagoon's MANTA Restaurant. In the evenings, the LOABI LOABI pool bar comes alive with parties, and for a more relaxed atmosphere while watching the sun go down, go on over to the KURUM-BAR.

The spa at Cocoon is the place to go if you want to unwind completely. Skilled spa therapists there use a wide range of treatments sourced from all over the globe to give visitors a luxurious spa experience that aims to heal them on all levels. You can't find a more affordable embodiment of chic sophistication than this.

Sun Siyam Iru Fushi Maldives
In addition to the assurance of total solitude, each of the spacious villas and retreats offers views of the seemingly endless ocean, perfect for watching the dawn or sunset. Outdoors, you'll find huge daybeds to sprawl on, swings to take in the sea breeze, and baths big enough to accommodate two people.

Indulge in a carefree stroll barefoot on the finest sand and unwind in the award-winning spa, or keep exploring until you discover a spot so secluded, you'll swear you've discovered an island all to yourself. And if you're seeking a more active vacation, the Maldives offer some of the top water sports in the world.

Raffles Maldives Meradhoo Resort

Raffles Meradhoo offers visitors the perfect blend of seclusion, tranquility, nature, elegance, and extreme luxury on the stunning Gaafu Alifu Atoll in the southern Maldives. The property also boasts impeccable service. Located in a tropical paradise, this colonial-era replica of the Raffles Singapore offers a refreshing change of pace from the usual Maldives hotels.

Aside from the pool in the water villa complex, there is another pool on the island. Additionally, you are welcome to take advantage of the free excursions to the house reef that a local marine biologist leads. Kayaks, SUPs, and snorkeling gear are all accessible to visitors at no cost, while jet skis and seabobs may be rented for an additional charge. Perched over the lake, you'll find a stunning gym with a glass façade. It's open all day, every day, and provides free yoga lessons.

A typical Balinese massage starts with the hum of a Tibetan singing bowl and concludes with the pouring of warm coconut oil into the so-called "third eye" to soothe the mind and promote sleep at the opulent overwater spa. Both of these things help reduce tension and get a better night's rest.

Soneva Jani

The Soneva Jani property's stunning blue lagoon offers a decadent escape that adventure seekers can't resist. Enjoy unparalleled access to thrilling watersports and marine activities from any of the resort's iconic over-water villas or spacious island apartments.

Nestled in the serene Noonu Atoll, embraced on all sides by sun-kissed azure skies and turquoise seas, is the five-star Soneva Jani resort. Among the world's lowest-density resorts, this one has only 51 over-water and 3 island villas. Every one of these enormous, exquisite villas in the Maldives has been meticulously designed to provide maximum seclusion, expansive living quarters, and breathtaking views of the ocean. Rent a water villa or an island villa and relax in the lap of luxury at this resort.

Conrad Maldives, Rangali Island

Set on two private tropical islands linked by a 500-meter footbridge, this unique resort is really one of a kind. Additionally, there is a standalone mansion with a master bedroom buried under the Indian Ocean and the first underwater restaurant in the Maldives can be found there. Guests won't have time to become bored because of the assortment of twelve eateries and bars, two spas, and activities.

Some of the recently renovated thatched-roof villas have individual gardens with pools or sunken baths; others are on stilts over the lagoon and include outdoor whirlpools or pools with stairs that go directly into the Indian Ocean. The spacious bathrooms with dual basins and Aromatherapy Associates products, together with the comfortable king-sized beds, cozy lounge areas, and floor-to-ceiling windows that let in natural light and create a calm, relaxing ambiance, make for an enjoyable stay.

Radisson Blu Resort Maldives

In the midst of the Indian Ocean is the Radisson Blu Resort Maldives, a five-star sanctuary where visitors may relax in elegant solitude. To ensure a smooth journey to the island where the hotel is situated, the experienced staff will arrange for all of your travel needs. While you're there, you may do scuba diving and snorkeling in some of the best places on Earth, and you can even encounter whale sharks in their natural habitat.

You may do scuba diving at the Dive and Water Sports Center, or you can visit one of the neighboring islands like Dhigurah or Maamigili. As you sip a glass of champagne from your villa's own pool, you may think back on your day exploring Fenfushi's coral reefs.

A fine dinner at one of the many restaurants serving cuisines from across the globe is the ideal way to cap off a memorable day. Grab a drink at the poolside bar or the beachside bar and relax with a view. Following a rejuvenating yoga session or a soothing massage at the Blu Spa, you and your loved ones may spend the day playing games or exploring the underwater world at the Dive and Water Sports Center.

You may find both of these establishments right there at the hotel. Take advantage of the complimentary Wi-Fi to share photos of stunning sunsets, delectable seafood dinners, and sandcastle constructions.

Nova Maldives

An all-inclusive resort with a community concept, NOVA Maldives champions Good Soul Days by providing unique, unforgettable opportunities for visitors to have fun while also reestablishing a connection with the natural world.

While there are many underwater excursions for aquaholics and those seeking wellbeing, some examples of these experiences include planting coral reefs and observing whales. They provide a vision of sustainable, meaningful luxury by allowing guests to swim with whale sharks and manta rays all year round and by encouraging them to build coral reefs in the hotel's garden.

In keeping with their commitment to community and culture, NOVA Maldives has introduced a new line of spa treatments modeled after traditional Maldivian Dhivehi Beys rituals. They will also be building upon their KULA Art Initiative, which hosts a series of workshops, pop-up exhibitions, and festivals to support and showcase the artistic abilities of locals, women business owners, and Maldivian artists.

This newest property, which debuted in June of 2022, is part of the Pulse Hotels and Resorts Group. It has 76 beautiful villas and provides visitors with a tranquil, joyful island getaway. For those who are interested in retreats, health, and ethical, environmentally conscious vacations, the newcomer NOVA has a lot to offer.

Sun Siyam Vilu Reef

Surrounded by some of the Maldives' most beautiful coral reefs are the water villas at Sun Siyam Vilu Reef. Unique plants and animals from all over the globe have called the resort's island home for over 20 years. While strolling to breakfast in the morning, you could hear the rustle of coconut trees and not be surprised to find a heron or hermit crab in the vicinity.

Slow down and indulge in some of the luxurious spa treatments, or choose to unwind in the seclusion of your own villa or apartment. In the evening, you can join the chefs as they showcase their creative and innovative meals. To top off a fantastic day, you can enjoy a private screening of a film under the stars.

JOALI Maldives

The main goal in designing the JOALI Maldives resort was to achieve sustainable elegance while simultaneously creating a beautiful, art-immersive island retreat. Renowned artists from across the globe and talented artisans from the region collaborated on the creation of this immersive venue. The Maldives as a whole benefit from their efforts to revive traditional handicrafts.

Muravandhoo Island, where JOALI is situated, is a portion of the massive and very deep Raa Atoll. Nestled in the extreme northern region of the Maldives is this region. Early geographers utilized the Divehi term "atholhu" to describe the region's distinctive ring-shaped coral reefs set inside placid lagoons; this is where the English word "atoll" gets its start.

The seventy-three large rooms, spread out throughout the lush island, redefine eco-chic luxury. Villas on the beach, villas on the water, and large mansions are all available.

Ayada, Maldives

Ayada Maldives is an exquisite resort with traditional Maldivian architecture and decor. The breathtaking private island where it sits is teeming with lush tropical flora and unspoiled beaches. With its several award-winning restaurants, large villas including private infinity pools, and luxurious AySpa, the Ayada Maldives is an excellent choice. Water sports, excursions, and a plethora of other exciting activities are available to guests.

The eight restaurants in Ayada Maldives provide a wide variety of cuisines and dining experiences, including teppanyaki, Mediterranean fine dining, and Asian. The authentic and deliciously fantastic food at these restaurants is made possible in part by the use of fresh, organic ingredients sourced from their own gardens and neighboring farms. Indulge in a one-of-a-kind experience pairing wine and cheese at Ile de Joie's over-water wine cellar. Customers with special dietary needs may be certain that their culinary staff is well-prepared to meet their needs.

LUX* South Ari Atoll Resort & Villas

If the idea of living a lavish island life à la Robinson Crusoe has ever crossed your mind, you have arrived at the right spot. Whale shark swimming, bicycling down the jetty, lounging in stilted bungalows, eight restaurants, nightlife, and marine conservation are all on the menu at LUX* South Ari Atoll. Indulge in all your favorite activities to the fullest at LUX* South Ari Atoll.

This resort is among the most romantic places you and your loved one can stay, and vacations are wonderful for strengthening relationships. The over-water villas Temptation and Romantic were both designed with couples in mind.

What about breakfast on a pool float? Have you ever thought about it? Is it midnight when you go swimming? Have your meal on a beach? That seems really fantastical, doesn't it? Anyone thinking about tying the knot for the first time or renewing an existing vow has come to the correct place. Their event coordinators would be more than happy to help.

Velaa Private Island

The dream vacation spot and place of ease were the original intentions for the villas on Velaa Private Island. After much deliberation and testing, they were finally ready for release.

Radka and Jimejc, a married couple, had a dream: to build Velaa Private Island, a private mansion and one of the world's most opulent private island resorts, in the Maldives, their favorite holiday spot. Located in the northern Maldives atoll of Noonu, Velaa Private Island offers an unparalleled and opulent island experience by satisfying the highest standards of seclusion, exclusivity, and luxury.

Czech architect Petr Kolar designed the private island, which, from above, looks like a sea turtle. On the island, you'll find a mix of private dwellings and 43 villas. A personal butler attends to all of the guests' needs. The resort has three restaurants run by the well-known chef Gaushan de Silva, a luxurious spa, and a golf course created by the illustrious José Maria Olazabal.

COMO Cocoa Island

Situated on a white-sand island in the center of a turquoise lagoon, COMO's private island getaway in the Maldives is a tiny and charming resort with 33 overwater villas.

The suites, which have one to three bedrooms and wooden walkways leading to them, take their design cues from the graceful curves of the traditional dhoni boats used in the area. A tranquil Maldives resort, the COMO Shambhala Retreat is perfect for recharging one's batteries. Views of the lagoon and the natural surroundings may be enjoyed from the treatment rooms. On top of that, they have one of the few hydrotherapy pools in the Maldives. This is a safe and effective method of massaging the body with high-pressure jets.

Located just forty minutes by speedboat from the international airport, COMO Cocoa Island offers unparalleled convenience.

Vakkaru, Maldives

Vakkaru Maldives is a secret coral island in Baa Atoll, a UNESCO Biosphere Reserve. The island has a house reef that is home to rare marine animals, powdery white sand dunes, deep blue depths, and views of the ocean that never fade. This picture-perfect paradise was meticulously constructed for travelers interested in epochal experiences, and it is accessible by a magnificent thirty-minute seaplane flight from the Male International Airport.

Whether you're traveling to the Maldives with a large group of friends and family or alone on a romantic retreat, Vakkaru Maldives has the most luxurious accommodations to suit your needs.

There is a plethora of private dining possibilities spread out around the island, in addition to the five restaurants, two bars, and wine cellars where you may savor delectable dishes from all over the globe, from Europe to Asia.

BEST BOUTIQUE HOTELS IN MALDIVES

Fairytale Inn, THODDOO

Fairytale Inn has free Wi-Fi, grilling facilities, a private beach area, and free private parking. It is located in Thoddoo in the Ari Atoll region. Thoddoo Beach is 800 meters away. This lodging has a terrace with views of the inner courtyard. In addition to a currency exchange and a 24-hour front desk, guests of the lodging may take advantage of full-day security. Each air-conditioned room at the guest home has its own private bathroom with a bidet, desk, kettle, refrigerator, safe, flat-screen TV, terrace, and security deposit box. Each apartment has a balcony with a dining space and views of the garden. Every room at the guesthouse comes with its own set of sheets and towels. Every morning, guests of the guest home may choose from a variety of breakfast selections, including continental and Asian dishes, as well as fresh fruit, pancakes, and pastries. You have the option to have groceries delivered on evenings when you would prefer not to eat out. Hikers and those interested in walking tours love the area around Fairytale Inn, where guests may also borrow bicycles for free. Guests of the inn may make use of the garden or go on bike rides in the surrounding area.

Boutique Beach All Inclusive Diving Hotel, DHIGURAH

The world-famous Dhigurah Marine Protected Area is home to whale sharks and manta rays, and the Boutique Beach All-Inclusive Diving Hotel is situated there. We provide free Wi-Fi. Guests may savor the breathtaking sunsets and safari boats from the Roof Top Boutique Heaven restaurant, which overlooks the Indian Ocean and our lagoon. Guests are provided with the convenience of a 24-hour front desk at Boutique Beach. You can reach the beach on foot in only a minute. In addition to air conditioning, each room here comes with a desk, a safe, and a balcony. The outside private bathroom has a shower and complimentary amenities. Guests may count on the PADI Dive Crew to gladly accompany them to the dive locations. Between Dhigurah and the island beyond it, there are fifteen deep reefs. With a three-kilometer stretch of natural sandy beach perfect for swimming and sunbathing, Dhigurah is about twenty minutes away by domestic shuttle from Male. Just ten minutes away by boat is the famous Kudarah Thila.

Coco Villa, THODDOO

Located in Thoddoo, Coco Villa offers a BBQ and views of the garden. Every accommodation has a private balcony, mini-fridge, electric kettle, flat-screen TV, and free Wi-Fi. Some rooms even include these extras. A hairdryer and complimentary toiletries are provided for your convenience. Biking, snorkeling, fishing, water sports, and scuba diving are all available on site, and the resort can even arrange a picnic on a secluded island or a romantic beachside meal. Located 70 kilometers away, Male International Airport is the closest airport to Coco Villa.

Sky Beach, Maldives, Dhiffushi

Sky Beach Maldives - Dhiffushi offers a private beach area, a restaurant, and a terrace only 600 meters from Dhiffushi Beach in Dhiffushi. Each room at this 4-star hotel includes air conditioning, free Wi-Fi, and a private bathroom; the hotel also has an outdoor pool. There is an ATM and room service available to guests at this motel. A closet is provided in each room at the hotel. Rooms at Sky Beach Maldives in Dhiffushi have flat-screen TVs, desks, and, in certain cases, balconies. Each guest room is equipped with a minibar for your convenience. Canoeing and other outdoor activities are available to guests of the resort in and around Dhiffushi.

Bliss Dhigurah, DHIGURAH

Bliss Dhigurah is a property in Dhigurah that has a private beach area and a sun deck. In addition to a restaurant and fitness center, this hotel also has a hot tub. We provide free Wi-Fi. Guests may make use of the hotel's bike rental service and water sports amenities. Adventures like scuba diving, fishing, and canoeing are all within your reach.

Among the Maldives' guesthouses, this one is among the most vibrant. A rooftop bar is also available.

Milaidhoo Maldives, BAA ATOLL

amid the vicinity of Hanifaru Bay, amid a UNESCO biosphere reserve, is the boutique luxury resort Milaidhoo Maldives. A world-class destination for scuba divers and snorkelers, its very own coral reef is off-limits to the general public. Handcrafted furniture and well-planned layouts draw inspiration from the Maldives. To satisfy all the senses, there are three eateries and two pubs. The picturesque island is encircled by a coral reef and surrounded by lush tropical vegetation. Its beaches are white and deep sandy. Each of the large, air-conditioned villas provides barefoot luxury with its own private pool of fresh water on the sundeck and extends out 180 degrees to let the island's natural beauty inside the villa. In every villa, you can see the ocean. An island host is available to take care of every aspect of the guest's stay, from scheduling spa treatments and excursions to filling the villa's private wine fridge with the guest's favorite bottles. With the Milaidhoo Gourmet package, you may enjoy all three meals a day along with a range of quality and international spirits, beers, wines, and cocktails. A personal island host is available at all times, along with a glass of champagne, a bottle of welcome gift, and access to a VIP airport lounge for both arrivals and departures. In addition to four treatment rooms, the floating spa offers free yoga and meditation sessions in its pavilion. Sailing, kayaking, catamarans, a 24-hour gym, and boat excursions are all part of the sports program. The facility offers dolphin tours, marine scientist-led conservation activities, whale shark sightings, manta ray viewings, fishing, diving, snorkeling, and more, in addition to an outdoor infinity pool. From Male International Airport, a picturesque 30-minute seaplane flight will take you to Milaidhoo. For an additional fee, the hotel offers airport shuttles.

The Mureed, FULIDHOO

Guests at the newly restored Mureed guest home in Fulidhoo have access to a garden and private beach. This motel has a restaurant, a 24-hour front desk, full-day security, and free Wi-Fi throughout the property, among other amenities. This house has a sun deck in addition to family rooms. Air conditioning, soundproofing, closet space, and a private bathroom with a walk-in shower are included in all apartments, which may be accessed via a private door. Each apartment has a balcony with a table and chairs for outside eating. Every room at the guesthouse comes with its own set of sheets and towels. The guest home offers both continental and American breakfast selections every morning. Guests may choose from a variety of warm meals, local specialties, and pancakes. In addition to offering packed lunches, guests are invited to relax in the on-site lounge. The Mureed offers complimentary yoga lessons to all guests. There is a baby safety gate, outdoor play equipment, and an indoor play space available to guests staying at this property. If you'd like to spend a day outside, the guest home has a picnic space

Island Break, FULIDHOO

Island Break in Fulidhoo has a garden and a secluded beach area. In addition to a sun patio and a restaurant that is suitable for families, this facility has a 24-hour front desk. Guests with disabilities may make use of the guest house's accessible rooms and family suites. Each room at the guest home has its own entrance and is soundproofed to provide a relaxing stay. Every accommodation has a private bathroom, a safe, and free Wi-Fi; some rooms even have patios and views of the ocean. Each room at the guesthouse has its own set of linens, including sheets and towels. In addition to packed lunches, there is a coffee shop on the premises. A children's playground is available to visitors staying at the guest home. This guest home has everything you need for a relaxing stay, including a picnic area and an outdoor fireplace.

Koimala Beach, Ukulhas, UKULHAS

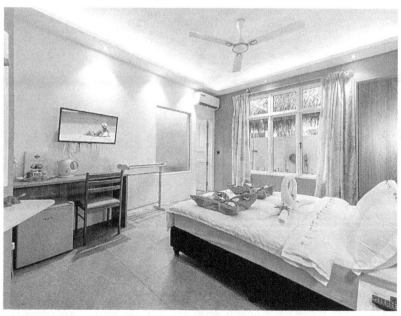

Just around 80 meters from Ukulhas Beach, the garden-viewing Koimala Beach Ukulhas offers complimentary bikes to guests. This motel has a restaurant, a 24-hour front desk, full-day security, and free Wi-Fi throughout the property, among other amenities. Guests of the lodging may make use of the establishment's currency exchange, room service, and concierge services. Air conditioning, a terrace with a dining area, and a flat-screen TV with satellite channels are all features of this air-conditioned property. A fireplace and sitting space are also included. Every morning, guests may choose between an à la carte meal and a continental breakfast that includes local specialties, pancakes, and fruits. There is a lounge for guests to relax in, and they can also have their lunches prepared. Within easy reach, you may get sightseeing trips. Guests at Koimala Beach Ukulhas may make use of the garden or go on local walking or biking activities.

Thoddoo Sunny Beach, THODDOO

Guests at the Thoddoo Sunny Beach may make use of the property's complimentary bikes, garden, communal lounge, and Wi-Fi. Room service, a 24-hour front desk, and currency exchange are among the amenities that guests can enjoy at this hotel. Each room at this hotel has a balcony that overlooks the garden. Guests get access to a hairdryer, complimentary amenities, and a private bathroom with a shower. Air conditioning and flat-screen TVs are included in all accommodations at Thoddoo Sunny Beach. Activities like snorkeling and cycling are available to guests of the resort in and around Thoddoo. In addition to standard business services like photocopying and faxing, Thoddoo Sunny Beach also offers an ironing service. Just 1.1 miles separates the hotel from Thoddoo Beach.

SeaLaVie Inn, UKULHAS

The SeaLaVie Inn is a Ukulhas lodging that has free Wi-Fi, a restaurant, and a BBQ. All of the rooms have flat-screen TVs. A sitting space is included in certain apartments, perfect for unwinding after a long day. In this room, you may locate a kettle. Private bathrooms are available in each room. Here, you may find complimentary toiletries and slippers for your comfort. At the facility, you'll discover a common lounge. You may enjoy water sports at this guest home, and there are bicycles available for free for your use. You may go snorkeling or scuba diving, among other things, in the region. At 73 kilometers away, SeaLaVie Inn is the closest airport to Male International Airport.

Ayala Ocean View, GULHI

In Gulhi, you can find air-conditioned rooms at Ayala Ocean View. Guests have the option to use a patio. Each room at this hotel has its own private bathroom, flat-screen TV, and closet. Guests will have the convenience of a fridge in each apartment. Continental and American selections are available for breakfast every day. The distance from Ayala Ocean View to Male City is 20 kilometers. Male International Airport is 22 km away, making it the closest airport to the resort.

Kagi Maldives Resort & Spa, NORTH MALE ATOLL

North Male Atoll is home to the 5-star Kagi Maldives Resort & Spa, which has beachfront views, an outdoor pool, a fitness center, and a garden. A private beach area and bar are just two of the many amenities offered by this resort. An Italian restaurant is available on-site at the hotel. There is free Wi-Fi available all across the hotel, a shared lounge, airport transfers, and a 24-hour front desk at this accommodation. Modern rooms with air conditioning, desk, coffee maker, minibar, safe, flat-screen TV, terrace, and private bathroom with shower are available to visitors at this resort. Towels and bed linen are provided in each accommodation at Kagi Maldives Resort & Spa. Every morning, guests have the option of a buffet, continental, or American-style breakfast. You may also ask for vegetarian, dairy-free, or halal alternatives. The Kagi Maldives Resort & Spa has a table tennis court.

Athiriveli, THODDOO

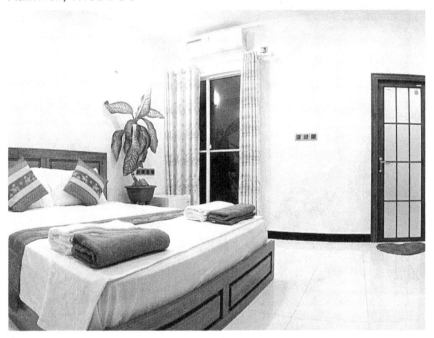

The Athiriveli in Alif Alif, Thoddoo, has a restaurant, grilling facilities, and more. Each room has climate control, a private bathroom, complimentary amenities, cable TV, and Wi-Fi. The guesthouse goes above and beyond to ensure that our guests have an unforgettable stay in Thoddoo by providing 24-hour customer service, a restaurant, a diving facility, and a water sports center.

PERLA Dhangethi, DHANGETHI

PERLA Dhangethi has a garden, a common lounge, and complimentary bikes. This resort has a restaurant and free Wi-Fi among its amenities. Guests may take use of the hotel's outdoor pool, exercise center, and round-the-clock front desk service. Air conditioning, sitting areas, flat-screen TVs with satellite channels, and private bathrooms with hair dryers and showers are included in all of the hotel's guest rooms. A desk and a kettle are standard amenities in every room. A buffet or an American breakfast are available to guests at PERLA Dhangethi. A patio is available with this hotel. Come to PERLA Dhangethi to play darts. Hotel guests may take use of the property's chargeable airport shuttle service to and from Male International Airport, which is located 88 kilometers away.

Each room at this boutique hotel is warm and inviting.

Fushifaru Maldives, FUSHIFARU

Just a 35-minute breathtaking seaplane ride from Velana International Airport lies the new, beautiful island of Fushifaru Maldives, on the far northeastern edge of Lhaviyani Atoll. The boutique and small Fushifaru Maldives resort is located in a diversified setting, with three of the Maldives' most prominent diving sites and a national Marine Protected Area bordering it. The resort offers an infinite promise of adventure, excitement, discovery, and tranquility. Each of the sixty-three beach and water villas at Fushifaru Maldives combines contemporary style with traditional Maldivian elements to create an atmosphere that is both cozy and magnificent. Gorgeous outdoor bathrooms with both indoor and outdoor showers, double vanities, daybeds, private verandas with eating spaces, and breathtaking views of the pristine lagoon and surrounding region are standard in each of the magnificent villas. A few of the villas even have their very own plunge pools. There is a wide variety of cuisines available, both local and foreign, to accommodate any palate or dietary restriction. Korakali offers mouth-watering breakfast buffets and delicious international food, Raakani serves up delicious surf and turf on the beach, and Teppanyaki provides an interactive dining experience. Enjoy the island's finest sunset views while sipping on a detox tail and a signature drink at Fanihandhi Bar's poolside lounge. Villa guests may enjoy a wide variety of foreign cuisines and snacks delivered straight to their room at any time of day or night. Private dining experiences including floating breakfast, poolside dining, and eating on the Handhu platform are also available upon request. At Above the Waterline, tourists and residents alike may enjoy a variety of recreational activities, including a fully-equipped gym with views of the Indian Ocean, a multi-sports court where matches are played often, a kids' club, and access to watercraft such as kayaks, catamarans, and jetskis. Next to the resort lies Below the Waterline - Fushifaru Kan'du, a national Marine Protected Area that has three famous diving spots, such as the world-famous Fushifaru Thila, which is rich in marine life and features unusual cave formations and a marine cleaning station. Wonderful place for snorkelers and scuba divers. Located only a short distance away in a pristine turquoise lagoon, the resort's own sandbank offers an unforgettable setting for weddings, picnics, and desert island retreats.

Outrigger Maldives Maafushivaru Resort, DHANGETHI
Among Maldives resorts, the Outrigger Maldives Maafushivaru Resort stands head and shoulders above the others. Set on a private island in the beautiful South Ari Atoll area, it is about 25 minutes via seaplane from Malé International Airport. The Outrigger Maldives Maafushivaru Resort stands out among all-inclusive resorts in the Maldives by

providing an experience that deftly blends the traditional Maldives with modern comforts, making it ideal for families seeking a romantic getaway or for couples hoping to reignite their romance. The island is short (just over 350 meters in length) and charming (only 10 minutes and a bit) because of its verdant foliage, powdery white sand, and house reef, which is home to a multitude of tropical fish. Villas with thatch roofs, which take design cues from the area, sit atop green gardens or jut out over the blue lagoon. All of the villas have immediate beach or sea access, and their deceivingly simple exteriors conceal a world of luxury. Allow us to assist you at Maafushivaru in creating treasured memories that will last a lifetime.

Komandoo Island Resort & Spa, Kamandoo

Favored by romantic partners. Located in Komandoo, the Komandoo Island Resort & Spa has a private beach area and a spa center. There is a bar available for guests' use. There is a flat-screen TV in every room. There is a sitting space in several of the apartments for your comfort. In this room, you may locate a kettle. All areas of the Komandoo Island Resort & Spa are equipped with complimentary Wi-Fi. The facility offers a variety of services, including room service, a tour desk, a gift shop, and a concierge. Activities like windsurfing and snorkeling are available to you.

Mirihi Island Resort, MANDHOO

Located in the South Ari Atoll in the Maldives, the tropical Mirihi Island Resort is named after a native flower. Guests may choose between beachfront or water villas and enjoy complimentary Wi-Fi throughout the resort and in each room. There are three different places to eat, and the water is very clear with stunning coral reefs. The rooms at Mirihi Resort include large outside lounging areas and polished wood floors. Each has a sun lounger, a CD player, and amenities for making tea or coffee.

Some even have views of the ocean. Upon request, we may provide you with a toothbrush and slippers. Male International Airport is about 85 kilometers away from Mirihi Island Resort. From the airport to the resort, the seaplane ride takes around 30 minutes. You may unwind with a massage at Duniye Spa and get in shape in the fitness center, which has all the latest equipment. You may find Chinese newspapers here. At the beach, you may do windsurfing or sailing, two water sports. Buffet fare at Dhonveli includes both local and foreign options, while at Muraka you can have Angus beef and fresh fish. At Anba Bar, you may have a drink.

Six Senses Laamu, LAAMU

A sustainable luxury resort, Six Senses Laamu is set in a picture-perfect location with white sand beaches and crystal-clear turquoise waters. A 37-inch flat-screen TV and a Bose sound system are included in each villa. The air-conditioned villas are beautifully appointed and come with an outdoor bathroom with a rain shower, so visitors can enjoy a refreshing shower while gazing at the stars. Guest rooms come with complimentary Wi-Fi. Guests may bask in the Maldives sunshine in the privacy of their own villa with daybeds and sun loungers. Room amenities include a dental kit, slippers, an electric kettle, and a full bathroom with a shower. Upon request, you may get a newspaper. Within the Laamu Atoll, located in the southern Maldives, there is the only five-star resort known as Six Senses Laamu. Olhuveli Island is 65 minutes by seaplane from Male International Airport, where it is situated. Ayurvedic treatments, soothing body massages, and chic individual treatment rooms are available at Six Senses Spa. In addition to a diving center and a yoga pavilion, the resort has a state-of-the-art fitness center. At LEAF, you may find contemporary Mediterranean meals made with organic, locally sourced ingredients, while at Altitude Wine Cellar, you can savor the finest wines and cheeses. We provide a variety of breakfast alternatives. Longitude serves up foreign cuisine; Sip Sip makes pizza; Ice sells ice cream; and the Chill Bar serves up cocktails.

BEST CHEAP & MID-RANGE HOTELS IN MALDIVES

The Residence at Dhigurah

The resort is worth the extra time and effort it takes to get here from Malé International Airport (a domestic flight south for an hour and a speedboat trip of fifteen minutes). Miles of shimmering white beaches, shapeshifting sandbanks, and bicycle trails through coconut groves make the most of the larger, longer, and more jungle-covered islands in the barely developed Gaafu Alifu Atoll, which is located just a stone's throw from the equator. The Residence makes full use of these features. We love the entry-level beach villas the most since they are huge, have a simple design, are quite private, and have their own pool. Overlooking verdant gardens and the ocean, you'll find The Spa by Clarins.

Kandima, Maldives

You can visit the remote Dhaalu Atoll, where the three-kilometer-long hockey stick-shaped Kandima sways over an unspoiled lagoon, on a budget by taking a local flight from the city. A stay here is less expensive than others since, unlike most Maldives resorts, this one also provides accommodations. Kickboxing, painting, and cooking courses are just a few of the many available activities. Other options include pool parties and stargazing movie nights.

Meeru Island

Families may be on the beach within an hour of landing at the airport jetty since this pleasant resort is nestled on a big natural island in a secluded section of the North Malé Atoll. Meeru is the largest island in the Maldives. In the middle of the island, you'll find a football field, tennis courts, badminton courts, and a golf course with a driving range and putting green. Two pools, two spas, five restaurants, three bars, and 286 garden, beach, or water villas decorated in vibrant colors are available elsewhere.

Sheraton Maldives Full Moon Resort and Spa
Only a fifteen-minute speedboat trip away from Velana International Airport, this expansive natural island has everything you could want: tennis courts, ping-pong tables, a water sports center, a kids' club, a holistic spa, and three pools (one of which has a waterfall). The four beachfront rooms in the most economical entry-level category each have a balcony or little sandy patio and are beautiful. The seven excellent

177

dining options make the most of your all-inclusive package; the Indian and Thai dishes are especially filling.

Kurumba, Maldives

The first resort in the Maldives is Kurumba. There were 30 simple apartments on the private island when it first opened in 1972; they were constructed from coral stone, palm thatch, and coconut wood. There was minimal power and the water for bathing was brackish. After 50 years, it has transformed into a chic retreat with 180 guestrooms, suites, and villas, eight dining options, a picturesque spa, and an exceptionally pleasant staff. The resort isn't as secluded as it once was, even though it's just a 10-minute speedboat ride from the airport.

Velassaru

From the capital, it's only a quick speedboat ride to the charming and stylish Velassaru. The island exudes an air of tranquility, with its wide expanse of powdery white sand providing enough opportunity for seclusion. The modern villas are bigger than usual and have unfussy flashes of color, dark woods, and pared-down taupes throughout. The living areas are split-level, and the bathrooms are monochromatic. After dark, go to Fen Bar for some meze and blue curaçao drinks while gazing out over the Indian Ocean and the infinity pool illuminated by LEDs.

The Standard Huruvalhi Maldives

The Standard, situated on the beautiful Raa Atoll and accessible by seaplane from Malé in just forty minutes, offers chic, designer furnishings, trendy eateries, and first-rate health and wellness services. Neon pink trims pale wooden cottages that have ukuleles hung on the wall, disco balls above the tubs, and flamingos inflated in the plunge pools. Also, there's a ton to do, including free yoga and pilates sessions, beach volleyball, swimming with manta rays, and dolphin-spotting excursions at sunset.

Constance Halaveli

The North Ari Atoll is a 30-minute seaplane ride from Malé, and the Constance Halaveli is a far more luxurious resort than its prices would indicate. The resort has a dive center, tennis courts, an infinity pool, an overwater spa, and restaurants with wine lists that have garnered accolades. Plus, an overwater villa won't break the bank, even though they're considered entry-level despite their large size, private plunge pools, and expansive decks with wooden stairs that go right into the baby-blue sea.

BEST HOSTELS IN MALDIVES

Dream Inn

In addition to its large deluxe rooms and family rooms, Dream Inn, one of the great locations to stay on Thulusdhoo Island, has an eight-mattress hostel. The three-star hotel is right on the beach, and it features a restaurant where you can have a hearty breakfast before you hit the sand. Free Wi-Fi is available throughout the neighborhood, and the helpful staff at the resort will arrange any kind of island excursion you can imagine. Truly a great spot.

Hanifaru Stay

Right on the oceanfront on the island of Kendhoo is a cozy bed and breakfast. Here, guests may enjoy some seclusion as they soak up some rays, thanks to the semi-private area. In addition, the guest house handles all transfers, which might be more cost-effective than other 1/3-birthday party options. In addition to offering non-smoking accommodations, the status quo also has a restaurant serving regional specialties. A stay for a really unusual amount of money.

Cokes Beach, Maldives

Situated right on the beach, the Cokes Beach Maldives is one of the best guesthouses on Thulusdhoo Island for surfers. Not only can you take basic surfing lessons from local pros, but you can also get snorkeling lessons here. The accommodations are clean and roomy, and the in-house restaurant serves breakfast and other meals. The area is managed by locals and aims to provide tourists with as authentic a Maldivian experience as possible.

Maafushi View

Maafushi is a beautiful island in the Maldives known for its palm tree-lined beaches and vibrant coral reefs. For a suitable and economical stay, choose the Maafushi View, a lodge-turned-hostel. The mattresses and towels provided are really comfortable, and when you rent a dorm room, you'll also get free amenities. Guests of this first-rate Maldives hostel may enjoy a complimentary light breakfast and can also ask the helpful staff about local tour options.

Rasdhoo Coralville

There are a lot of tourist-oriented tours that this establishment is known for. The seashore is marked with many spots where you may go surfing, snorkeling, diving, or fishing. The accommodations are large and clean, the restaurant is available for your meals, and the staff is helpful and kind. There is a babysitter service available for guests, and the place is great for families. It was generally thought to be a pleasant experience by those who were there.

CHAPTER SEVEN

10 MUST EAT PLACES IN MALDIVES: WHERE TO EAT IN 2024

With its seemingly endless ocean, the Maldives—a group of coral islands in the middle of the Indian Ocean—has long been lauded for its unparalleled beauty. Indulge your taste buds at one of the many wonderful restaurants in the Maldives, nestled within this breathtaking natural landscape. If you're looking for an unforgettable dining experience, the Maldives has it all. From the best seafood served on beautiful beaches to the excitement of eating underwater among colorful aquatic creatures, there's something for everyone.

1. Reethi Restaurant

Guests of this Maldives restaurant may enjoy a breathtaking view of Reethi Beach as they dine. While the waves are lapping at the coast, savor a variety of foreign dishes and seafood that has just been caught. After dark, Reethi's beautiful over-water veranda transforms into a vibrant theater of cuisine, and the restaurant is famed for presenting an extensive brunch menu. Indian curries and Thai dishes are also available for tasting. Reethi is one of the top restaurants in the Maldives because it serves food made using traditional methods using original recipes.

Location: Maldives
Opening Hours:
Breakfast: 7 am to 11 am
Dinner: 7 pm to 10 pm
Cuisines: Pan-Asian, modern European

2. Pebbles by Royal

The largest restaurant at the Royal Island Resort, Pebbles By Royal, offers breathtaking views of the ocean and delectable dishes. Indulge in a delectable combination of Asian and Mediterranean cuisines at this hidden treasure in the Maldives. Pebbles by Royal is likely to fulfill any appetite you may have, whether it's for a Mediterranean meal or something more exotic. Among the top restaurants in the Maldives, the

Pebbles provides an opulent dining experience with its sea breeze-served platters. Indoor or outdoor seating is available as an option.

Location: Dhadimagu, Maldives, Genmiskih Magu, Fuvahmulah 18018, Maldives
Opening Hours: 9 am to 12 am
Cuisines: Asian fusion and Mediterranean

3. The Market

Among the best restaurants in the Maldives, The Market is located in the Dusit Thani Maldives and is a gastronomic paradise. From traditional Maldivian fare to popular dishes from across the world, this restaurant has it all on its buffet and à la carte menus. Dine al fresco beneath the stars at one of these Maldives honeymoon spots for a really memorable supper. If you're looking for a diverse and pleasurable eating experience in the Maldives, The Market is a great option since it caters to a broad range of preferences.

Location: 634M+6RG Dusit Thani, 06180, Maldives

Opening Hours: Everyday, 7 to 11 am, and 6:30 to 10 pm

Cuisines: International and Maldivian Cuisine

4. Maaniya Restaurant

In Nalaguraidhoo, at the Villa Park Sun Island Resort, you'll find Maaniya Restaurant, whose flavor fusions will transport your taste buds. For those who love seafood, this Maldives beachside restaurant has an irresistible array of fresh catches and foreign dishes. Every dinner at this Maldives restaurant is an unforgettable experience because of the warm atmosphere and friendly service. Every palate may be satisfied at this restaurant, whether you like foreign cuisine or local specialties.

Location: Nalaguraidhoo, Maldives

Opening Hours:

Breakfast: 7:30 am to 10 am

Lunch: 12:30 pm to 2 pm

Dinner: 6:45 pm to 9 pm

Cuisines: Seafood and Maldivian cuisines

5. The Spice

The Spice, located inside the Atmosphere Kanifushi Maldives, serves a vivacious fusion of Asian and Indian cuisines. Among the most alluring things to do in the Maldives, eating here offers an immersive experience with its savory tastes and environment that affords stunning ocean views. A variety of tasty delicacies are available for you to enjoy in a cozy setting. One of the best Indian restaurants in the Maldives, The Spice, will take your taste buds on a gastronomic whirl with its explosion of delicious Indian spices and breathtaking ocean views.

Location: Atmosphere, Kanifushi Maldives, Kanifushi Island, Lhaviyani Atoll, Maafilaafushi, Maldives

Opening Hours:

Breakfast: 7 am to 10:30 am

Lunch: 12 pm to 2:30 pm

Dinner: 7 pm to 10 pm

Cuisines: Asian, European, and Maldivian

6. Hot Rock

The Hot Rock restaurants on Meeru Maldives Resort Island provide a unique dining experience unlike any other in the Maldives. In addition to the exhilarating water activities and relaxing on the sun-kissed beaches, you may also prepare your own food at your table using hot stones. Take your eating experience to the next level with an interactive experience that lets you customize your meal to your liking. Hot Rock is one of the top Maldives restaurants, and for good reason: the views of the ocean are breathtaking, and you can hear the sizzle of your food as it cooks on a hot stone.

Location: FP39+884, Dhiffushi, Maldives

Opening Hours: 11 am to 6 pm, and Dinner: 7 pm to 10 pm

Cuisines: Italian, Maldivian

7. Ithaa Undersea Restaurant

The Ithaa Undersea Restaurant at the Conrad Maldives Resorts is the most renowned and spectacular underwater eatery in the Maldives. In this restaurant, you may enjoy fine meals while taking in breathtaking views of the ocean's marine life. Dine underwater for an unforgettable and surreal experience while taking in the stunning views via the glass walls. Muraka is more than a restaurant; it's a portal to the underwater marvels of the Maldives.

Location: Conrad Rangali Island, 20077, Maldives
Opening Hours:
Lunch: 11 am to 2:30 pm
Dinner: 6:30 pm to 10:30 pm
Cuisines: European, Seafood, Oriental

8. Sea Fire Salt

Reimagine beachside dining at Sea Fire Salt, a gourmet seafood grill at Anantara Dhigu Maldives Resort. This eatery offers delectable steaks and seafood with a view of the Indian Ocean. With its unique combination of ingredients and presentation, every dish is a culinary masterpiece. For a memorable romantic dinner for two on the Maldives islands, Sea Fire Salt is the place to go for a touch of opulence and a pinch of romance.

Location: XGF2+5GC, Anantara Dhigu, Gulhi, Maldives
Opening Hours:
Lunch: 12.30 noon – 2.30 pm
Dinner: 6.30 pm – 10.00 pm
Cuisines: Seafood

9. Terra at Waldorf Astoria

An awe-inspiring treetop dining experience is offered by Terra at the Waldorf Astoria Maldives, Ithaafushi. Indulging in a meal at one of the most intriguing restaurants in the Maldives while perched high above the verdant foliage is an experience in and of itself. Enjoy an exquisite wine list accompanied by a gourmet meal with a wide range of tastes. Indulge in a delectable gastronomic adventure at Terra, where the stunning landscapes of the Maldives come alive. Those in search of an unusual atmosphere to complement their gourmet dinner will find it to be an ideal retreat.

Location: Ithaafushi Island, Male, 20009, Maldives
Opening Hours: 7 am to 10:30 pm
Cuisines: Austrian, Contemporary, Laotian, Mexican, Sushi, Tunisian

10. Thila by Kurumba

At Kurumba Maldives, you'll find Thila, a restaurant that fuses foreign and local tastes. In a casual and welcoming atmosphere, you may savor

194

a variety of meals, from seafood to international specialties. Beautiful live music, gentle ocean breezes, and an outside setting make this Maldives restaurant all the more appealing. Especially on special occasions like the Maldives New Year's Eve, take in the mesmerizing atmosphere and live entertainment held under the starry canopy. Thila assures a great eating experience that satisfies a variety of preferences, whether you're yearning for foreign delicacies or a taste of Maldivian culture.

Location: 6GGC+HGQ, Vihamanaafushi, Maldives
Opening Hours: 7am to 11 am, and 7 pm to 9:30 pm
Cuisines: Seafood, European, International, Grill, Contemporary

EAT LIKE A LOCAL IN MALDIVES: 10 MUST-TRY FOODS

Because Maldivian food is so diverse, it could be difficult, if not impossible, to sample every single dish in a single lifetime. If you're looking for a nutritious and flavorful cuisine that you've probably never heard of, try Maldivian food. Local cooks use rice, seafood, coconuts, and fragrant spices to make delectable dishes that will blow your mind with their array of flavors.

Visiting Male or one of the nearby islands is the best opportunity to sample authentic Maldivian food. At the Maldivian evening buffet, which numerous five-star hotels host, you might find your new favorite food. However, the restaurant on your island probably serves some of our favorites. If you order it with some sides, rice (which is usually included), and dessert, you won't be disappointed.

Here are some of our favorite recipes from our time in the Maldives, ranging from beachside traditional fare to more homey takes on Maldivian flavors.

1. Mas Riha (Maldivian Fish curry)

In the Maldives, Mas Riha is a popular curry dish that goes well with rice and Roshi, a flatbread. This is a staple lunch and supper for the locals.

This rich and creamy recipe usually calls for coconut milk, fresh chiles, cinnamon, a blend of spices, and pieces of chopped tuna. The Maldivian fish curry, one of several regional recipes showcasing this unusual mix of staple ingredients, made it onto a CNN list honoring the global development of curries.

2. Mas Huni

Without trying the native food, your beach vacation in the Maldives would be lacking something. In the Maldives, mas-huni, a combination of tuna and coconut, is the most popular breakfast item. Combine smoked tuna with a puree of onion, capsicum, lemon juice, and salt; stir in the coconut pulp. To complement the meal, roshi bread is served. Roshi is sometimes used to bake Mashuni. Masroshi is the name given to this delicacy, which is basically spherical pies that are golden and have a crust.

At Tasting Table, the resort's main restaurant, you may have this simple but delicious Maldivian breakfast dish called Disc Mashuni, which is pronounced as Disc Mas-huni. Mas huni goes well with your standard black tea. It is highly discouraged to consume any kind of liquid, even fresh juices. The Tasting Table serves delectable dishes from across the world, in addition to traditional Maldivian cuisine. In a tranquil setting, such as a seaside patio or dining room, you may savor delectable dishes from throughout the world, from Asia to Europe.

3. **Garudhiya (fish soup)**

You ought to give this dish a try if you like miso or dashi. Delicious traditional Maldivian fish soup with a fragrant boil and a hint of lemon. In addition to being the soup's primary component, fresh tuna also imparts a significant taste. The fish cubes are simmered in a curry leaf, onion, garlic, and chili broth before being garnished with fried onions and lime juice that has just been squeezed.

Despite its seeming lack of complexity, garudhiya is great for cooling down in the winter and serving as a refreshing soup in the summer.

4. Bis Keemiya (samosa)

Bis Keemiya tastes like a cross between a curry puff, samosas, and rolls. Pastries that are light and flaky, filled with chopped cabbage, tuna, eggs, hard cheese, spicy onions, and a great chew. They are softly cooked. This meal stays true to its fiery and salty roots while highlighting the fundamentals of Maldivian cuisine with its prominent use of tuna. You won't believe how light and tasty they are until you try them. Prepare for maximum flavor when served hot.

Stuffing Bis Keemiya with whatever toppings you desire—including vegetarian options—makes it taste even better, and it's quite simple to make. If you are seeking a taste of the traditional and genuine cuisine of the Maldives, you will not have any trouble finding this dish at any of the five-star resort restaurants.

5. Boshi Mashuni (Banana flower salad)

Crushed, blanched (but still crunchy) banana blossoms, fresh coconut, and spices make up boshi mashuni, a dish that falls between salad and salsa. The limes bring out the best in this dish, which is already fiery from the onions and Maldivian chilies (or ordinary chilies; just make sure they're as sharp as a bird's eye) and has a zesty undertone from the curry leaves, turmeric, and cumin. Even though it has nothing to do with delicious food, the dish's exceptional healthfulness is a major selling point.

6. Saagu Bondibai (sago pudding)

Has it been a while since you had sago? On the other hand, the Maldives rely on these little starchy balls—made from the spongy centers of tropical palm stalks—as part of their daily diet.

Sago is still a staple in Maldivian cooking, and when you have saagu bondibai, you'll see why. Indulge in generous servings of this warm dessert made with coconut milk, cardamom, rose, and creamy condensed milk for every meal of the day.

7. Banbukeylu Harisa (bread curry)

Breadfruit, a tropical fruit that is both delicious and versatile, may be cooked into a curry or served as a sweet treat. Once you get over the sticky part of practically peeling off the fruit, you'll be able to taste its robust and nourishing flavor.

The Maldivian bread dish known as Banbukeylu Harisa is a crowd-pleaser. Curry stays true to traditional Maldivian cuisine by skillfully blending smoked tuna, breadfruit, coconut milk, and a myriad of spices into a delectably rich and flavorful dish. Hot or cold, this meal goes well with roti, rice, or fresh bread. You could eat only the curry and be satisfied.

8. Rihaakuru

Rihaakuru is mostly a thick paste made with fish. The food's hue might vary from pale brown to a deep, rich brown. As one of the archipelago's traditional foods, it has been enjoyed almost every day in Maldivian homes since ancient times. Pair the spaghetti with your favorite grains for a satisfying meal. It is also a common ingredient in many other spice blends. One must exercise caution not to ingest too much pasta due to its highly acidic composition.

A by-product of processing tuna is rihaakuru. After hours of simmering in a mixture of salt and water, the tuna is cooked until it flakes easily, a procedure that is both easy and laborious. After the tuna reaches the desired doneness, it is taken out of the oven and either eaten or kept. These fried fish pieces will undergo further processing to create the world-renowned dried Maldivian fish. Boil the remaining fish stock and "bondi," or tuna byproducts, until all the water has disappeared. The end product is a thick paste called Rihaakuru in the Dhivehi language.

9. Kulhiboakibaa

An integral component of Maldivian cuisine for countless generations, Kulhiboakibaa (kuliboakibaa) is a traditional fish cake. Traditionally served during island-wide holiday festivities, this dish is finding new fans as an accompaniment to afternoon tea these days. To make the cake, you'll need a thick rice paste, some tuna, some spices, and some young and old coconut.

10. Dhonkeyo Kajuru

Maldivian sweet tooths may satisfy their cravings with Dhonkeyo Kajuru, also known as Donkeyo Kachuru. Made with flour, sugar, bananas, and coconut, it's a delicious treat. The dish is a deep-fried banana pancake or ball variation that is very sticky and sweet, with crunchy bits. This meal doesn't necessarily need to be enjoyed at a street food stand. This delicacy, which is offered in many restaurants on several islands, has a particular taste that is enhanced by the vanilla that is incorporated in the banana puree.

THE 12 BEST MALDIVES CLUBS & BARS

You have entered the mesmerizing realm of Maldives nightclubs, where paradise and entertainment converge to provide an experience, you will never forget. This magnificent island in the middle of the Indian Ocean has a thriving nightlife that will keep you entertained for days. After dark, the clubs light up with the music of DJs from all over the world, creating an electric atmosphere. The Maldives is home to some of the world's most beautiful nightclubs, where you may dance the night away accompanied by the soft sound of the ocean wind or beneath the twinkling stars. Indulge in exciting water activities and scuba dive to see colorful coral reefs. You may meet other travelers at these clubs, which is a great way to make friends and have fun. The clubs in the Maldives will immerse you in their beauty, joy, and adventure.

1. Subsix

Situated six meters below the water's surface, Subsix is a Maldives underwater nightclub. Incredible sea vistas surround this extraordinary location, which provides an otherworldly and wonderful experience. As you dance under the waves to the pulsating music, you'll see a rainbow of marine life pass past. The combination of the hip vibes and the breathtaking underwater scenery makes for an amazing experience. Indulge in a one-of-a-kind party trip at Subsix, a real wonder that blends the beauty of the ocean with throbbing sounds.

2. Aura Nightclub

Famous for its spectacular theme parties and interesting events, Aura is a popular nightclub in the Maldives. The large, energetic dance floor will transport you to another universe where music and dancing are the soundtrack. Live DJs with a wide range of musical talents keep the party going all night with their varied sets. At Aura, you may quench your thirst with one of their many cocktails as you soak up the lively ambiance. Aura is the place to go for a once-in-a-lifetime night on the town, so brace yourself for the mesmerizing atmosphere and contagious energy.

3. 1 Oak Lounge & Bar

Perched on a private Maldives beach club, 1 Oak Lounge & Bar creates the perfect atmosphere for a sophisticated and fashionable evening. Where sophistication meets entertainment, you'll find this chic venue. Famous DJs set the tone for an amazing night of celebration with their mesmerizing rhythms. The club has a lively vibe that keeps the excitement going, and the live acts will captivate you. As you dance the night away, sip on one of many quality drinks or one of many well-made cocktails. An oasis of opulence and entertainment in the middle of paradise, 1 Oak Lounge & Bar is the pinnacle of sophistication.

4. The Beach Club

Stylish and lively, The Beach Club is located on the picturesque island of Kanifushi. Live music, seaside parties, and exciting events attract throngs of people looking for a once-in-a-lifetime night out at this hip venue. As entrancing music from a variety of skilled performers fills the air, you can't help but feel the night's rhythm. As the gentle touch of the seaside air envelops you, dance under the twinkling stars. If you're seeking a vibrant and exciting atmosphere, the Beach Club is the place to go for a thrilling night on the town in paradise.

5. Babuna Bar

Babuna Bar is a haven of peace and beauty on the beautiful Kuramathi Island. This delightful spot is well-known for its easy-going vibe, which provides a peaceful retreat from the everyday. Sit back, relax, and take in the tropical scenery as you sit on the beach and feel the soft ocean air on your skin. With live music providing a relaxing atmosphere, Babuna Bar is the ideal setting for lazy times. With karaoke nights thrown in, it becomes even more entertaining and exciting for those who are looking for a little more energy. Learn to unwind like a pro at Babuna Bar, where the pace of life slows and worries disappear.

6. Coco Bar

Enter a secret paradise on an island, where the magic of Coco Bar comes to life on balmy nights. Offering a serene environment reminiscent of a hidden paradise, this magical sanctuary serves as an entrance to rest and connection. Live music and skilled DJs will create an energetic ambiance as dusk approaches, infusing the air with lyrical rhythms that will transport you to another world. Watch as expert bartenders create a wide array of mouth-watering drinks as you indulge in the science of mixology. Coco Bar's allure is hard to refuse; it entices people to come and enjoy the nightlife while making memories that will last a lifetime.

7. Kuredu Island Resort Disco

Kuredu Island Resort, located in the beautiful Lhaviyani Atoll, is home to a lively disco where you may start your rhythmic adventure. As you enter this vibrant haven, you'll be transported to a world of throbbing rhythms and contagious vitality. Guests may dance the night away to the newest tunes played by skilled DJs at this disco, which is a paradise for music fans. Themed parties raise the energy level to a frenzy, making for an electric environment. The Kuredu Island Resort disco guarantees a memorable experience that will have you moving and grooving, whether you're looking to groove to your favorite songs or immerse yourself in the lively atmosphere.

8.   F Club

Greetings and salutations from the beautiful Paradise Island in the Maldives, home of the world-famous F Club nightlife. Enter a room that exudes a contagious sense of style and modernity. Live DJs at F Club skillfully choose a wide variety of musical styles to satisfy any crowd, setting the mood for an amazing evening. F Club has music for all tastes, whether you like soft R&B melodies, infectious pop songs, or throbbing techno sounds. In the midst of an energetic group of partygoers, let the music transport you as you dance the night away. An unforgettable and thrilling experience awaits you at the F Club, right in the middle of paradise.

9. Liquid Nightclub

Located on the picture-perfect island of Velassaru, Liquid Nightclub is the place to go for an exciting night out on the town. In this other world, the dance floor is your playground and the beats are in your blood. The dynamic music in this lively club contributes to its electrifying atmosphere. With their incredible themed evenings and special events,

Liquid Nightclub guarantees that every visit is an unforgettable and exhilarating experience. Immerse yourself in the music, dance to the rhythm, and enjoy the electric atmosphere of Liquid Nightclub.

10. Deep End Club

Deep End Club is an enchanting location on Meeru Island, where you may lose yourself in the lively atmosphere. Going all in on fun and excitement is what this club is all about, as the name says. Enter the euphoric dance floor, where the music will make your heart skip a beat. The karaoke sessions are the perfect place to let your voice shine while also making new friends and having a good time. Every night at Deep End Club is different and memorable, thanks to the crowd-pleasing live entertainment. Prepare to enter a world of limitless joy and make memories that will last long after the last note has played.

11. Club Med Kani

Club Med Kani, a tropical oasis in the stunning Maldives, is the epitome of adventurous luxury. Indulge in a variety of thrilling activities at this private island resort, which provides a one-of-a-kind partying experience. Club Med Kani is known for its exciting beach parties and live DJ performances. Indulge in mouth-watering drinks while dancing under the starry sky and soaking up the lively ambiance. Daytime activities include windsurfing, kayaking, and snorkeling among the beautiful coral reefs.

Immersed in breathtaking natural beauty, Club Med Kani guarantees a memorable night of clubbing.

12. Sundown Bar

Sundown Bar is one of the elite Maldives clubs that provides a magical, carefree nightlife experience, and it's located on a perfect length of beach. This coastal haven comes to life when the sun sets, painting the powdered sand and blue waves in a golden light. Sundown Bar is the perfect spot to chill with a drink in hand and some exotic music playing in the background. The calm atmosphere is ideal for having private conversations or simply admiring the breathtaking Maldivian sunset. Sundown Bar is the perfect place to unwind and enjoy the enchantment of the evening with its laid-back vibe and breathtaking views.

CHAPTER EIGHT

BEST MALDIVES BEACHES TO VISIT

Landaa Giraavaru

The picture-perfect beaches of Landaa Giraavaru, one of the Maldives' most sought-after private islands and home to a Four Seasons resort, are the epitome of opulence. A lengthy sandbank stretching into the ethereal blue lake awaits visitors at this location. The Four Seasons describes the beaches of this idyllic island as "a natural UNESCO Biosphere Reserve wilderness where iridescent blues, jungle greens, and dazzling whites meet innovation, conservation, and wellness with equal, vibrant intensity." The cherry on top is a living reef just waiting to be discovered, along with sea turtles, manta rays, and other marine life.

Baros

Unspoiled beaches border Baros Island, and the island's crystal-clear seas and coral reef give the already-unparalleled scenery an otherworldly quality. Stay at Baros Maldives, the exclusive resort on this private island, to explore the tranquil Baros beaches. The venue goes above and beyond by arranging intimate candlelit meals on the powdery beach.

Reethi Rah

Guests at One&Only Reethi Rah get exclusive access to some of the Maldives' most exclusive beaches, which are located on Reethi Rah. Reethi Rah has twelve secluded and stunningly lovely beaches spread out over its 3.5 kilometers of stunning coastline. Because it is in its own time zone, one hour before Malé, it is also home to some of the Maldives' most breathtaking sunsets. In addition to providing villas with immediate beach access, One&Only will also arrange for sun loungers on the beach for families who want to spend the day relaxing.

Veligandu Island

Veligandu Island is where you'll find soft sand, overwater bungalows, and a seemingly endless sandbar. Guests of the adults-only Veligandu Island Resort & Spa in North Ari Atoll are the only ones allowed on this beach. In addition, the area is large enough that each hotel guest will get the impression that they are on their own private beach. Luxurious thatched-roof pavilions and loungers line the beaches, and the water's many colors of green and blue are caused by the coral that surrounds the island.

Thulusdhoo Island

Thulusdhoo, a surfing paradise in the Maldives, is the capital of the Kaafu Atoll. Some local hotspots, like Thulusdhoo, allow tourists to experience the real culture of this idyllic archipelago, in contrast to the

219

numerous islands in the Maldives that are home to magnificent five-star hotels. From Malé, you may reach Thulusdhoo on a cheap boat that takes around 1.5 hours. The island has a wide range of hotels to accommodate different budgets. Beachgoers in need of some rays can visit Tourist Beach, while surfers in search of the biggest waves should make their way to Cokes Beach.

Hulhumale Island

Hulhumale, an artificial island in the North Malé Atoll, is a real place in the Maldives. With its more commercial and Westernized vibe and bustling hotels, shops, and restaurants, it provides a drastically different experience compared to many other islands in the archipelago. The charming beaches of Hulhumale are perfect for a weekend getaway, and the area is teeming with beachside restaurants, shops, and water activity providers. Indulge in a day of snorkeling, paddleboarding, or just relaxing on the beach with a beverage in hand.

Fulhadhoo Island

Only 250 people call Fulhadhoo Island, which is far longer than it is broad, home in the Baa Atoll. The island is characterized by tranquil blue lagoons and little natural ponds that grow along the shore. Fulhadhoo, a haven for a wide variety of fish, dolphins, and turtles, is a stunning location for scuba divers and snorkelers. Beautiful and serene, only two hours by speedboat from Malé, this island is perfect for nature lovers and wildlife enthusiasts alike. Its beaches are mostly deserted, and visitors have a good chance of seeing exotic animals.

Ukulhas Island

Ukulhas is a little-known island in the Alif Alif Atoll that has beautiful, clean beaches that are regularly cleaned to attract tourists and fight pollution. Resorts on the island span all price points; most are within walking distance of the beach, but none have direct access. Still, visitors flock to the island for the beach—a perfect one-kilometer length of white sand dotted with umbrellas and beach loungers. You can always find a spot to relax on the beach since it is both peaceful and large. With its affordable rates and picture-perfect Maldivian beach, Ukulhas is a great option for vacationers of all means.

Omadhoo

Omandhoo is a peaceful island in the South Ari Atoll that is only now beginning to establish its tourist attractions. There are 800 people living in the town, which occupies almost 60% of the island. Visitors that are interested in respectfully learning more about local culture will love the environment of the island, which seems truly Maldivian due to the low prevalence of Western habits. The beaches on Omadhoo are peaceful and uncrowded, and beachgoers will like the lengthy sandbank that stretches out into the pristine ocean. Turtles, whale sharks, and schools of fish (such as snapper and barracuda) call the reef that surrounds the beaches home.

Dhigurah Island

About sixty miles off the coast of Malé is Dhigurah Island, which is part of the South Ari Atoll. Visit this island if you want to see whale sharks, do scuba diving, and relax on beaches you won't want to leave. Dhigurah, similar to Thulusdhoo, has a number of hotels and popular places for both tourists and residents to hang out. There are picnic tables on the gorgeous Dhigurah sandbar, a diving facility on the island, and sea turtles and many colorful fish congregate in the water around the little sugar-sand beach.

Hadahaa

Located on an island in the North Huvadhoo Atoll, the Park Hyatt Maldives Hadahaa has a 360-degree house reef that encircles the whole island. Protected by Park Hyatt's sustainability commitment to maintain a healthy reef, clean waterways, and beaches and limit their total environmental effect, these beaches are screensaver-worthy with their pristine white sand and enticing blue waters. Green Globe and a marine scientist on staff keep an eye on these beaches to make sure they don't go along with the rest of the Maldives' most beautiful coastlines.

ROMANTIC PLACES IN MALDIVES: SPOTS TO WOO YOUR PARTNERS

Manta Point

If you're planning a scuba diving honeymoon in the Maldives, make sure to include Manta Point in your itinerary. If you're looking for a thrilling water adventure activity in the Maldives, this is the place to go. Get ready to have an incredible time while getting up close and personal with the local marine species. Upon your arrival, you will find a great deal of work to do.

Although the rental equipment might be somewhat pricey (up to USD 100 per person), the experience is really unforgettable. Scuba divers should definitely make the trip, and honeymooners will love it for all the unique experiences it offers.

Once your basic training is underway, you will be able to effortlessly dive deep into the water, allowing you to observe the ocean depths and experience life here. Before you go into this task, double-check that you fully grasp all of your guide's directions.

Situated in North Male Atoll, Lankanfinolhu Island

Bandaara Kilhi Lake

As the Maldives' biggest freshwater reserve, Bandaara Kilhi Lake is a breathtaking natural attraction. A thicket of tropical almond, cheese fruit, banana, coconut palm, taro, and mango trees encircle it. Ferns and screw pine trees also make an appearance. Additionally, this area is home to a wide variety of unique critters and species, in addition to its verdant vegetation.

Some of the wildlife that calls the lakeside home are the Maldivian white-breasted waterhen and the common moorhen, both of which are unique to the Maldives archipelago and Fuvahmulah in particular. Because of this, it is considered one of the best honeymoon spots in the Maldives.

Location: Bandaara Kilhi, Fuvahmulah (Ghazee Magu)

Dhadimagi Kilhi

227

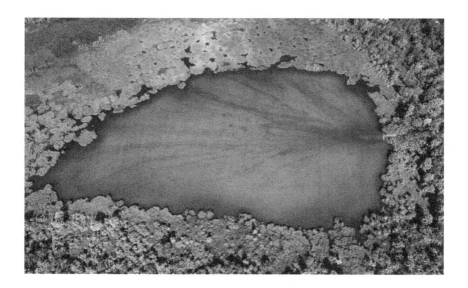

In the same area as Bandaara Kilhi, there is another lake called Dhadimagi Kilhi. Here you may find a wide range of flora and fauna, including some bird species that are at risk of extinction on a worldwide scale. If you're looking for a place to go hiking where you can hear the unique songs of birds as you explore the diverse ecosystem of uncommon plants and trees, this may be the place for you.

Because these places are so important, the government has done an excellent job of restoring and conserving them so that they may serve as tourist attractions that people from all over the globe can readily enjoy. If you want to witness a variety of plants and animals that you won't see anywhere else on Earth, you have to visit this lake.

Location: Fuvahmulah, Maldives
Banana Reef

The North Male Atoll's Banana Reef is another interesting attraction. As the name implies, you will be able to see the abundant animals flourishing within the verdant foliage of banana plantations. Still, that's not all. The scuba diving routes in this region are legendary, and once you're underwater, you'll fall head over heels for them.

This is due to the fact that taking that leap into the deep water will allow you to see a vast array of marine life and animals. When getting here isn't hard, the incredible underwater sights you'll experience when scuba diving here will take your breath away. A honeymoon to the Maldives would not be complete without visiting this stunning location.

This attraction is a must-see. Once you've seen the stunning Banana Reef for yourself, the words you read here will seem like old news. The underwater scenery is so picturesque that it will stay with you forever.

Located in the North Male Atoll in the Maldives, Banana Reef

HP Reef

A more accurate name for HP Reef would be the bewitched reef. Girifushi Thila and the Rainbow Reef are two other well-known names for it. Dive in and allow the breathtaking scenery to take your breath away. The HP reef is an undersea wonder so stunning and fascinating that no amount of reading can do it justice. Witness it firsthand.

The newlyweds can't go on their honeymoon without stopping here. With its lofty trees, graceful branches, vistas adorned with shoreline, and the magnificent sunrises and sunsets that can be seen from every spot, this place is a visual feast.

Location: North Male Atoll

The Grand Friday Mosque

A notable architectural structure in Male is the Grand Friday Mosque. With a capacity of more than 5,000 worshippers, the mosque is not only the biggest in the Maldives but also one of the biggest in all of South Asia—something that is hard to fathom on the tiny island nation. This building serves several vital purposes beyond just being a place of worship and education.

Several offices, an Islamic library, and a conference hall are also available at the center. It is also the site of formal ceremonies and events. Because of its stunning design and proximity to Male's main dock, the mosque also serves as a popular stop for sightseers.

This further enhances its accessibility from several directions. One of the distinctive features of the region is the spectacular golden dome of the mosque, which is clearly visible on the skyline of Male. The mosque is a historically significant place in terms of art and architecture, with its gleaming golden dome and interior walls covered with stunning wood carvings and Arabic calligraphy standing out.

The creative landscape of the Maldives has evolved, as seen here as well. In addition to the conference room and library, the center offers a number of resources for learning about the site's history.

Location: Ibrahimee Magu, Corner of Medhuziyaarai Magu, Male

Tsunami Monument

A steel monument studded with spheres commemorating individuals who lost their lives in the 2004 Boxing Day tsunami stands at the Tsunami Monument in Male. The fact that the locals here honor the militia and veterans is just one more reason why this is a must-visit location for honeymooners interested in Maldives history.

Location: Thin Ruh Park, Boduthakurufaanu Magu, Male

The Hulhumale Mosque

With its spacious interior, the Hulhumale Mosque was built in the 2000s and can house over 1500 worshipers. For a more modern and fusion-inspired look, this mosque incorporates elements from a number of different art forms and design schools into its construction. In honor of Sheikh Qasim bin Al-Thani, the mosque bears his name. Near the hospital, to the northeast of Hulhumale, you may find it.

Location: Hulhu Male' Vaguthee Mosque, Asar Maa Hogun, Maldives

Alimatha Island

Alimatha Island is a paradise for ecotourists and marine life enthusiasts. Because of the wide variety of things to do, this is definitely one of the Maldives honeymoon spots that no couple should miss.

Myaru Kandu, a popular diving spot on this island, is considered by the Maldives government to be among the country's safest. Any level of expertise may benefit from it. Here in the deep waters of the Indian Ocean, they love scuba diving with all sorts of fish and marine life. The residents often enjoy short vacations on this island to escape their regular lives.

Location: Eastern Edge of Maldives, Vaavu Atoll
Distance from Male: approx. 65 kilometers

Biyadoo Island
Biyadoo Island is a lovely getaway in and of itself, offering budget-friendly access to the Maldives' top attractions. On the other hand, you'll

have access to a plethora of extravagant amenities within walking distance at the COCOA resort. Because of its abundance of world-renowned diving spots, this Maldives island is also known as a scuba diving island. The abundance of banana, coconut, and mango trees on this island provides lush vegetation and a vibrant atmosphere.

There is no shortage of famous faces at this COCOA resort; it is the Maldives getaway of choice for many A-listers. You could just see your favorite star basking in the sun and sand right here, so be ready to swivel your head and gasp every few minutes. Among the top Maldives honeymoon spots, this one has suddenly soared to the top!

Location: South Male Atoll
Distance from Male: 29 kilometers

Aarah Island

Due to its low population density, Aarah Island in Vaavu Atoll is the Maldives' most secluded destination. This is the perfect spot for newlyweds who want complete seclusion on their honeymoon, since the population is fewer than 100.

Just Park yourself here and enjoy the peace and quiet if you're looking for some alone time. Once you reach the island, you'll have peace of mind as you take in the breathtaking views of the ocean, coastline, and surrounding vegetation.

Location: Vaavu Atoll
Distance from Male: 155 kilometers

Bikini Beach

When planning a honeymoon to the Maldives, this is a great spot to go. No honeymoon would be complete without a visit to Rasdhoo's Bikini Beach, as the name implies. It is well-known among couples for its white beaches and the facilities it offers.

This beach is home to the Rasdhoo scuba dive club and dive facility, where the happy couple may have an out-of-this-world underwater adventure. Everyone is welcome to jump in, regardless of swimming ability, since the instructors are very skilled. The most appealing aspect is that the government has gone to the trouble of dividing the beaches according to dress code and other restrictions.

Location: Maafushi:
Distance from Male: 60.8 kilometers

Lily Beach

As one of the Maldives' most opulent resorts, Hulahendhoo's Lily Beach is a popular choice for honeymooners. Seen from Male, this resort is easily accessible by seaplane across the Alifu Dhaalu Atoll, so getting there is a breeze.

If you're in a position where money is no issue, you should visit this elite resort at least once in your lifetime. Each suite has its own terrace and outdoor Jacuzzi so the newlyweds may relax in peace and quiet throughout their honeymoon. Unspoiled house- reefs a few meters from the coast, verdant tropical flora, and pristine beaches all contribute to the island's well-deserved reputation.

Location: Hulahendhoo, Maldives
Distance from Male: 87 kilometers

Bandos Beach

You can enjoy everything the beach has to offer without breaking the bank at this beach, making it ideal for those on a tighter budget. Prices on this beach range from one hundred to two hundred dollars. Located in the middle of Bandos Beach, North Male Atoll is a popular diving site with over 40 dive spots. This island is ideal for divers and offers a variety of opportunities to see marine life; it should be a part of any Maldives honeymoon package.

Location: North Male Atoll
Distance from Male: 9.9 kilometers

TRAVELING ON A BUDGET - MONEY SAVING TIPS

To travel without breaking the bank, one must be strategic and prepare ahead. To help you enjoy your vacation without going into debt, here are ways to save money:

Plan and Research in Advance:
- Find inexpensive lodgings, inexpensive things to do, and inexpensive restaurants by doing extensive research on your location.
- Get a head start on finding cheap airfare, hotels, and activities.

Travel During Off-Peak Seasons:

- If you want to save money on airfare and hotel rooms, plan your trip during the off-season.
- There will be fewer people, so it will be less expensive and more pleasant.

Flexible Travel Dates:

- Allow some leeway with the dates of your trip. Sometimes, you may save a lot of money on flights and hotels if you change your plans by only a day or two.

Use Public Transportation:

- Instead of using a cab or a rented vehicle, use the bus or train. It's a great way to save money and immerse yourself in the local culture.
- Tourists may get reasonably priced public transit passes in several locations.

Stay in Budget Accommodations:

- Think about staying in inexpensive hotels, hostels, or vacation rentals rather than five-star hotels.
- You may discover a variety of possibilities for economical hotels on websites and applications.

Cook Your Own Meals:

- Make some of your own meals at home to cut down on restaurant bills. If you'd like the option to prepare your own meals, look for lodgings that feature kitchenettes.

- In order to get fresh and affordable foods, peruse the nearby marketplaces.

Pack Snacks and Water:
- Bring your own snacks to save money on those pricey snacks sold in tourist areas.
- Bring a refillable water bottle to keep yourself hydrated all day long.

Free and Low-Cost Activities:
- Find out what free or cheap things to do in your location, like going to museums on days when admission is half off or attending outdoor concerts.
- Oftentimes, walking tours are both inexpensive and educational, so be sure to take advantage of them.

Use Travel Apps and Loyalty Programs:
- To get the most affordable flights, hotels, and activities, use a travel app.
- Join loyalty programs to earn points and savings with your favorite airlines, hotels, and rental car businesses.

Currency Exchange and ATM Fees:
- Keep an eye on the exchange rates and look for trustworthy local institutions to exchange your money at for the best deals.
- To prevent paying exorbitant withdrawal costs, use ATMs prudently. For a list of partners that provide fee-free withdrawals, contact your bank.

Travel Insurance:

- Insurance for your vacation might help you save money in the event of a medical emergency, trip cancellation, or misplaced baggage, even if it seems like an extra cost.

Pack Light:

- Choose carry-on luggage and pack little to avoid paying more for baggage.
- If you pack wisely, you may save both time and money since many low-cost airlines charge more for checked luggage.

With these budget-friendly suggestions, you may have a once-in-a-lifetime vacation without breaking the bank. Always put your most important priorities first when allocating funds.

CHAPTER NINE

7 DAYS IN MALDIVES: AN ITINERARY FOR FIRST-TIME TRAVELERS

Embark on a 7-day adventure holiday in the Maldives that combines culture, luxury, and more. This vacation will be one you won't soon forget, what with sightseeing in Malé, diving, and eating at an underwater restaurant.

Day One: Explore Malé & Experience Local Life

The capital of the Maldives, Malé, will be your first stop on your itinerary. A full-day walking tour will give you the rundown of the area, and it comes with lunch, a knowledgeable local guide, and the opportunity to donate to a local NGO called Save the Beach.

Relax with supper at a trendy neighborhood joint after a day of sightseeing.

- **Morning**

  At Meraki Coffee Roasters, you can start your first day in Malé with a small breakfast and gourmet coffee. The personnel at this neighborhood coffee roaster are warm and welcoming, and the shop itself is chic and contemporary.

  Gather at Jetty No. 5 to meet your guide for the full-day walking tour of Malé once you've had an opportunity to fill up. Touring the majority of Malé's top attractions is only the beginning; your knowledgeable guide will also fill you in on the history, politics, and culture of the Maldives.

  By seeing the Malé Fish Market, you may get a better understanding of the cultural and economic significance of fishing in the Maldives. Make sure to inquire about the top fish dishes to eat at the restaurants in Malé while you're there.

- **Afternoon**

  As part of your walking tour, you will eat lunch, so you may try some of the local market food. Stopping for afternoon tea with your guide is another opportunity to sample some authentic Malé delicacies. During Ramadan, the tour will not be offering any snacks or treats.

- **Evening**

  The Cloud Restaurant will be the perfect place to unwind after a day of sightseeing in Malé. Perched on the tenth floor, this neighborhood hangout provides diners with a breathtaking panorama of the city and its waterways.

Guests may enjoy a variety of cuisines at The Cloud Restaurant, incorporating some Maldivian flavors with their worldwide favorites.

One of the most beloved dishes is the tuna steak. The restaurant isn't quite cheap, but it does have fair rates compared to others in the vicinity. The Cloud Restaurant follows the policy of many Malé establishments and does not offer alcohol.

Day Two: Daytime Swimming & Sunset Fishing

On day two of your Maldives vacation, take in the sights along Malé's stunning coastline before venturing out on a boat for a new viewpoint. Fishing for tropical fish as the sun sets is the ideal way to round off a beautiful day.

- **Morning**

  A delightful small restaurant located only feet away from the Tsunami Monument, Cypress Café and Bistro is the perfect place to start your day with breakfast.

  The typical Maldivian breakfast is served at reasonable pricing at the charmingly local Cypress Café & Bistro. Western breakfast favorites, including eggs Benedict, waffles, and shakshuka, are available for those who desire them.

  Villingili is a little island off the coast of Malé; when you've fueled up, take the boat there. Be careful to check the timetable before you set out so you can plan your return travel, although generally speaking, the boat operates throughout the day. Spend the remainder of your day discovering the tranquil seas and easygoing atmosphere of the little island of Villingili.

- **Afternoon**

  The water at Villingili Public Beach is a vivid shade of blue, making it an ideal swimming place. You could even meet some Maldivians at this public beach, as it is well-liked by both visitors and residents.

  Relax in the peaceful streets of Villingili and stop by one of the cafés for some hedika, or Maldivian tapas, when you're ready to take a breather. If you're looking for a fast lunch before your sunset fishing cruise, Hedika is usually served between 3 and 5 in the afternoon.

Take the boat back to Malé when you've had enough time to swim and explore Villingili. Traveling to Hulhumale in time for your evening trip is essential, so give yourself plenty of time. Taking a cab from Malé's downtown to Hulhumale takes about 20 minutes.

- **Evening**

  Join a sunset fishing excursion from Hulhamale and cast your line for the tropical fish that inhabit the waters around Malé.

  As you wait for the fish to bite, take in the breathtaking vistas of the Maldives' shoreline and the Indian Ocean. Anyone, from seasoned fishermen to complete novices, may enjoy this exciting pastime.

  The boat provides snacks and beverages, but if you want to have a BBQ for dinner, you'll need to make a reservation in advance. The trip does not include dinner, so be prepared to spend more for that. There is no alcohol in the beverages that are served.

Day Three: Beach Day & Underwater Photoshoot

On the third day of your Maldives vacation, you'll have a hearty breakfast before heading to the museum and, finally, the beach. If you want to have lasting memories of your vacation to the Maldives, hiring a professional photographer is a great option.

- **Morning**

  Breakfast at Seagull Café will set the tone for the day. This restaurant is unlike any other, thanks to the enormous tree that grows right in the center of the dining room.

  The staff is warm and helpful, and the menu includes pancakes with fresh fruit, smoothies, and traditional Maldivian food.

  The National Museum of the Maldives is the next stop on your itinerary; you'll have passed it on your first day of sightseeing in Malé. An hour or two here will give you a good sense of the Maldives' culture and environment as you peruse the displays and learn about the island's marine life.

- **Afternoon**

  Relax on one of the breathtaking Maldives beaches. Hulhumale Public Beach stands out among the other beaches with its picture-perfect white sand beaches and crystal-clear blue seas. After you've had your fill of the breathtaking scenery, go on over to Eastern Beach.

  Engage a local photographer for underwater photography if you want really stunning images to cherish as a memento of your journey. You and the people you care about will return from your trip with images of the highest quality, perfect for sharing with friends and relatives or printing off for posterity.

  If you want your vacation images to really stand out and capture the wonder of your adventure, hire a professional photographer.

In addition, you will get a professionally produced 60-second film that you can easily post online or gift to loved ones.

- **Evening**

The Maldive Kitchen serves delicious, traditional Maldivian food. There is a set menu at this eatery, and the cuisine is both delicious and humble. On top of that, the Maldive Kitchen has a stellar reputation for its welcoming and helpful personnel.

The spicy and aromatic curries served at the Maldive Kitchen are a hit among guests. During certain seasons, you may also get regional delicacies, such as screw pine juice.

The restaurant is on the smaller side; therefore, a reservation is a must. Customers have complained that the service is sluggish, so this isn't the place to go if you're in a rush for your meal.

Day Four: Snorkeling Safari & Stargazing

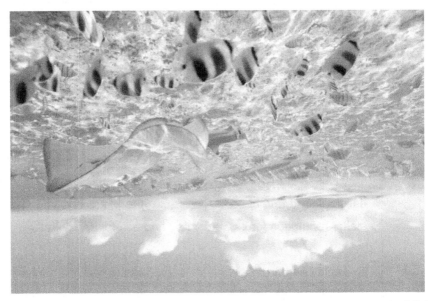

Go on a full-day snorkeling excursion and discover the many tropical fish that inhabit the Maldives and their delicate habitat. A sunset dolphin cruise is the perfect way to cap off a day of amazing fun.

- **Morning**

  Before your tour of Malé begins, have breakfast at your hotel or a nearby restaurant. After that, set off for Hulhumale in your vehicle or a cab for your full-day snorkeling adventure.

  On your trip, you'll have the option to swim with tropical fish or just rest beneath an umbrella in the shade. In order to help you learn about the marine creatures you see while snorkeling, the tour will supply you with fish identification cards.

  You get a buoyancy aid and all the gear you need to go snorkeling. An experienced local guide will accompany you throughout the day and be happy to fill you in on all things Maldivian and the islands.

- **Afternoon**
  Huraa, a neighboring island where you may view a new Maldivian island, will be your lunch stop. After that, we'll go back out to sea to see the rays, sea turtles, and reef sharks that call the islands home.

You will have several opportunities to see vibrant marine life since the experts are familiar with the top snorkeling locations in the region. With a maximum of eight people per tour, you'll have plenty of opportunity to interact with your guide and ask them questions.

Sunset dolphin cruises are the perfect way to round off the day. An unforgettable experience awaits you as you see the playful dolphins playfully jumping and swimming in the vicinity of the boat.

- **Evening**
  Try the Thai cuisine at Sala Thai or go back to one of your favorite Malé eateries for supper. Known for its delightful and genuine Thai classics served in a warm and inviting setting, this restaurant is next to the Sala Boutique Hotel. Head to the beach (or the pool at your hotel if it's too far away) after supper to see the stars.

Incredible stargazing is possible in the Maldives at night. Light pollution in the Maldives is far lower than in most other places, so you may enjoy a clearer view of the breathtaking night sky while you're there. Guests of Helengeli who like stargazing may also take advantage of the island's more secluded beaches to do just that.

Day Five: Visit Helengeli Island & Stay In An Overwater Villa

OBLU NATURE Helengeli All-Inclusive Resort is where you'll spend the fifth day of your Maldives vacation. Staying in an overwater villa in the Maldives will allow you to gaze out over the crystal-clear ocean while you relax and unwind.

- **Morning**

  Savor your last meal of the day in Malé at your hotel or a local favorite. Perhaps you'd want to have a last cup of coffee at Meraki Coffee Roasters or take a last walk on the man-made beach.

After you've had your fill of Malé and said your goodbyes, go north to the North Malé Atoll to OBLU Nature Helengeli. Amazing snorkeling and scuba diving possibilities abound at this resort because of its house reef, which encircles the island.

Notify the resort in advance of your departure time from Malé so they can organize transport for you. It takes around half an hour by speedboat to get to Helengeli.

- **Afternoon**

  Your vacation can really begin after you've had the opportunity to settle into your villa at OBLU NATURE Helengeli. A kind greeting, some water, and face towels will make you feel right at home the moment you step foot in the door.

  Next, make yourself at home in your villa. Overwater villas designed like dhonis, the traditional Maldivian boats, make up the Lagoon Resort.

  You have the option to jump straight into the sea from your balcony or take a leisurely walk down the wooden jetty that links you to the rest of the resort.

  Perhaps by now you've become used to the late afternoon Maldivian snack, or hedika, that you eat on a regular basis while on vacation. From 4 to 6:40 pm every day, the Hedhikaa Hut serves traditional appetizers.

- **Evening**

  The Spice is OBLU's on-campus restaurant, where you should have your meal. Desserts, Maldivian specialties, and world cuisines come together at this casual eatery.

  Guests may savor a unique assortment of meals and specialty beverages every Friday during Indian Ocean Nights. Listen to a DJ or live band perform after supper. At OBLU, you may enjoy entertainment five evenings a week, with Friday being reserved for movie night.

  As part of their all-inclusive plan, OBLU allows you to enjoy an unlimited supply of food and beverages, including alcohol. The resort's trademark drinks are OK, but they won't entice you to stay here.

Day Six: Water Sports or Diving From Helengeli

You have the opportunity to partake in watersports or go scuba diving on your last day in the Maldives. Helengeli and the surrounding region are famous as prime diving spots in the Maldives, but if you'd rather remain on the surface, you may engage in both motorized and non-powered water activities.

- **Morning**

  If you're looking for a way to get some movement and stretching in before the sun rises, try a morning yoga class by the pool. Otherwise, go on over to the Spice, OBLU's onsite restaurant, for an early breakfast. The next day, you'll be spending the whole day on the water.

  Divers can use OBLU to plan a dive trip that lasts a few hours or a whole day. It is highly advised that you make a reservation for the scuba diving experience well in advance of your desired date. This will allow the OBLU group to organize with TGI Dive & Water Sports Centre.

  Many marine animals, including manta rays, octopus, turtles, and reef fish, may be seen when diving from a boat. Another option to take into account is night dives, when bioluminescence illuminates the water.

- **Afternoon**

  You may either keep diving or try out some of the aquatic activities offered by the resort. Guests may enjoy the resort's array of watercraft throughout their stay, including kayaks, stand-up paddle boards, pedals, and snorkeling gear.

  Paddleboarders and kayakers may glide over Helengeli's pristine blue waters, pausing to admire the vibrant schools of fish that swim by.

  Renting jet skis and zipping around the lagoon is a fun way to get some speed. You can also go parasailing, waterskiing, wakeboarding, flyboarding, or knee boarding.

  An afternoon line fishing expedition is included in your stay, which may be the ideal way to spend it on Helengeli.

- **Evening**

  A sunset cruise aboard a dhoni, a traditional Maldivian boat, is an option if the weather permits. Shooting a few images can help you remember the event.

Then, having lunch at the resort's restaurant, Spice, is a must. Visit Helen's Bar for a taste of island nightlife while taking in breathtaking views of the lagoon. From Helen's Bar, you have the option to go snorkeling along the reef or just have a refreshing swim in the lagoon.

Gather some beverages from the minifridge in your villa and locate a quiet place on the beach to watch the stars as night falls. If the weather holds, astronomy at Helengeli should surpass that of Malé.

Day Seven: Relaxing Spa Day & Underwater Dining

The OBLU NATURE Helengeli resort is the perfect place to unwind on your last day in the Maldives. After indulging in a relaxing spa day, treat yourself to a spectacular underwater restaurant for dinner.

- **Morning**

The onsite restaurant, Element X, offers delicious breakfast options influenced by Western, Central Asian, and Far Eastern flavors. In addition to coffee and juice, there are baked products and pastries to choose from.

Following that, you are free to roam the island at your leisure, taking in the stunning coral reefs, verdant landscapes, and beachcombing beaches. You may swim in the pools, lounge on the beach, or wade in the ocean; the decision is yours.

- **Afternoon**

  Indulge at OBLU NATURE Helengeli's ELE | NA spa, which focuses on organic and sustainable practices. A variety of soothing services, including manicures, massages, and facials, are available to you.

  Ayurvedic massage, yoga, and meditation are all part of the Journey to Holistic Wellness program, which is one example of a traditional Maldivian therapy.

  In any case, you may return to your villa feeling revitalized and ready to take on the world.

  Indulge in some last-minute pool time or beach lounging after your treatment in the Maldives. Snorkeling over the reefs or even just having a drink at the bar may fit into your schedule.

- **Evening**

On your last night in the Maldives, treat yourself to an unforgettable dinner at the underwater restaurant Only BLU. In a one-of-a-kind atmosphere with schools of inquisitive tropical fish swimming about, Only BLU serves you amazing contemporary food.

Sharks have been seen swimming past several diners. The outstanding service at the restaurant will elevate this once-in-a-lifetime occasion to new heights by going above and beyond to make your experience unforgettable.

You should be prepared to pay extra for the dinner at Only BLU, as it is not included in the OBLU NATURE dining package. Make sure you get a table at the restaurant by making a reservation in advance if you want to dine there.

Made in the USA
Monee, IL
17 December 2024

74027928R00144